Recipe for Creating a Peaceful Classroom
A Guide Book for Early Educators

Dr. Tamara Pelosi

Dr. Tamara Pelosi

ISBN: 198613590X
ISBN-13: 978-1986135900

DEDICATION

I dedicate this book to all the Early Childhood Educators making a difference in children's lives.

Tamara Pelosi

Dr. Tamara Pelosi

Dr. Tamara Pelosi

CONTENTS

Recipe for Creating a Peaceful Classroom: A Guide Book for Early Educators

By: Dr. Tamara Pelosi

Teacher & Child Poem

"I have come to the frightening conclusion that I am the decisive element in the classroom. It is my personal approach that creates the climate. It is my daily mood that makes the weather.

As a teacher I possess tremendous power to make a child's life miserable or joyous. I can be a tool of torture or an instrument of inspiration; I can humiliate or humor, hurt or heal.

In all situations, it is my response that decides whether a crisis is escalated or de-escalated, and a child humanized or dehumanized."

Haim Ginott

Dr. Tamara Pelosi

Dr. Tamara Pelosi

ACKNOWLEDGMENTS

I have been blessed with an amazing supportive family and an awesome circle of friends, without their support I doubt if I could have made it to where I am today.

Thank you, Pam Allen, Stephanie Dockweiler and Kathleen Johnson, for taking time out of their busy lives to read the manuscript, sometimes more than once, and for their constructive suggestions.

Thank you, Joanne Romano, for our long walks and continued support and encouragement along the way.

Thank you Lonni Campbell for your professional guidance.

Special thank you to my mother for all that you do and have done for me, especially helping my vision of this book become a reality. Thank you for your endless encouragement in helping me not to give up through all the obstacles that I was confronted with. Thank you. Thank you. Thank you. I love you.

Dr. Tamara Pelosi

Foreword

Recipe for Creating a Peaceful Classroom: A Guide Book for Early Educators by Dr. Tamara Pelosi is a must have, must read for anyone working in an early childhood classroom with children Birth through 3rd grade. I have known Dr. Pelosi as a friend and colleague for over 15 years. Her passion and dedication to the children, staff, and families that she has worked with is unparalleled. Dr. Pelosi's book comes at a critical time in our society that is filled with violence, unkind people, and unkind words. Although many of us might live in our own little bubble thinking that the effects of the world don't touch the lives of young children, we are sorely mistaken. Children are arriving to early care and education programs with challenging behaviors that teachers are not equipped to deal with. The effects are staggering. Twelve years ago, Yale University researchers uncovered a surprising fact: Preschoolers were more likely to be expelled because of challenging behaviors than children in any other grade. In fact, preschoolers were being expelled at rates more than three times higher than school-aged children.

Recipe for Creating a Peaceful Classroom is a step by step process that needs to be a requirement for anyone working with young children. It focuses on the skills that teachers need as well as the skills that children need to be taught. In the United States if a child doesn't know how to read, we teach them, if a child doesn't know how to write, we teach them, but if a child doesn't know how to behave our first reaction is to punish them. This book outlines Dr. Pelosi's methods using social emotional guidance, the understanding of child development, the power of self-awareness, the purpose of making intentional connections, as well as using conflict resolution in the classroom with young children.

The time for this book has come. I encourage you to pick this book up, read and absorb the content and try the strategies and tools outlined by Dr. Pelosi. It will change the way you work with young children and the way you think about children in general. Good luck in your work with young children. Remember, you are making an investment in the future.

Stephanie Dockweiler, MS
Owner/President QS2 Training and Consulting

"Be the change you want to see in the world."

Mahatama Gandhi

Introduction

"There is no such thing as a bad kid, only kids with problems that need help in resolving them." (Gartrell, 2002). This quote resonated with me the first time I read it.

While working in the early childhood field, teachers often complained about a problem child, or "this bad kid" they had in their class. This negative feeling towards a child didn't sit well with me. I firmly believed the children weren't bad, they were merely misunderstood. I knew there was much to be explored, discovered and taught. My gut told me to focus on the "why" and not the "what" of behaviors. The subject fascinated me so much that I chose to research challenging behaviors and the correlation to teacher training in my Doctorate Program. My dissertation was titled, *"Increasing Social-Emotional Skills in Aggressive Preschoolers by Training Preschool Teachers in an Improved Teaching Methodology."* My hypothesis explored the strategy that if early educators were trained and educated in why challenging behaviors occur and given the tools and logistics to deal with them, there could ultimately be a peaceful classroom. Thus, "Recipe for a Peaceful Classroom" was born.

It is reported from early childhood educators that each year more children with challenging behaviors are enrolled in their classrooms, a problem for which they perceive a need for assistance if they are to help these children (Bryant, Vizzard, Willoughby & Kupersmidt, 2000). When children in my research sample exhibited challenging behaviors and limited social skills, their teachers stated they felt frustrated, stressed, angry and helpless at times. Teaching children with emotional or behavioral problems is one of the most perplexing and challenging jobs in education (Cheny & Barringer, 1995).

Due to the increase of working parents and single-parent households more children are enrolled in daycare centers. Children from a very young age are separated from their parents for many hours, leaving both parent and child exhausted by the end of the day. The perfect storm for teachers facing challenging behaviors.

Time and again I hear early childhood educators state they need more patience. It is true that patience is an important factor when working with children, but it is not merely patience that will create a peaceful atmosphere, it is understanding.

What Educators Need:

- Understand the appropriate developing behaviors for each age and stage.
- Understand how to implement developmentally appropriate practices in the classroom.
- Understand how the brain develops and the impact of a positive or negative environment.
- Become familiar with how some of the risk factors may look.
- Learn how to prevent and de-escalate a behavior.
- Learn how to remain calm.

- Know the goals of a behavior.

- Understand the power of self-awareness and cultivating communication skills.

- Learn not to take a child's behavior personally.

- Learn how to problem-solve and build the appropriate skill.

- Know the importance of providing a predictable and structured. routine with choices to create the number one need – SAFETY.

- Understand how connection is the key.

It is vitally important for the early childhood educators to equip themselves with the above ingredients because, once you understand, practice and employ them, patience is not as crucial because you have a recipe full of ingredients.

The goal for this book is to provide a guide for early educators on how to implement a comprehensive approach for understanding and responding to challenging behaviors that are exhibited in a classroom. The ingredients for this approach are richly rooted in researched child development, brain development, developmentally appropriate problem solving, proactive strategies, intervention techniques, self-awareness, tools and the peaceful classroom's values and principles. Implementing this approach creates a safe and cooperative setting where children are free to investigate the world around them while the teachers marvel at the wonders of the children.

Listed are the ingredients that were created from over twenty years of research in the field of

Early Childhood. Each ingredient is extremely important and builds upon the others, creating a peaceful classroom.

Peaceful Classroom Ingredients

1. Power of Self-Awareness

2. Richly Rooted in Knowledge

3. Creating a Safe Environment

4. Communication Skills 101

5. Intentional Connection

6. Social-Emotional Learning

7. Conflict Resolution in the Classroom

8. Understanding Challenging Behaviors

9. Problem-Solving Challenging Behaviors

To inspire learning we need to reach more than the child's mind, we need to reach their heart as well. The willingness to be open to a new approach for understanding challenging behaviors by proactive practices, self-reflection, and a non-judgmental environment will assist in creating the peaceful classroom.

When you are educated you will be the instrument of inspiration. It takes heart and it takes the extra step.

Ingredient #1: Power of Self Awareness/Calm

"All you can change is yourself, but sometimes that changes everything."

Gary Goldstein

Ingredient Self-Awareness/Calm

Early childhood teachers are known for spending every ounce of energy they have taking care of the needs of others. As rewarding as this is, sooner or later the body and the mind become depleted, and when that happens there is little or nothing left to give to anyone. It requires tremendous energy to be a positive leader in a classroom of rambunctious little ones. Those in the nurturing field need to take care of themselves first, physically and emotionally. It is imperative for every human being, and especially for those who work with children, to get ample rest, eat nutritious meals, exercise, allow even a few moments of peace and relaxation, socialize with friends and family, and keep the brain stimulated with intellectual pursuits. **This is not selfish - it is essential.** Think of the metaphor - put your oxygen mask on first! When teachers bring the best of who they are to their roles, they have the focus and clarity to embrace all aspects of their work. The lasting benefits will be felt in every facet of the program and most of all by the children. It all starts from Self-awareness.

Self-awareness is your emotional intelligence, as Daniel Goleman states. It is the first step to any kind of change. It is your ability to be conscious of your thoughts, perceptions, strengths, weaknesses, passions, limitations, triggers, values, habits, feelings, and actions. In order to understand others, you first must understand yourself. At times you can go through life on auto pilot, going through the motions of the day. But more often we need to stop and be mindful of our actions, tone of voice, and the way we respond. We need to act with mindfulness, not on impulse and habit. Habit can be comfortable even when it is a negative habit. Developing self-awareness will help in every aspect: in the classroom, with co-workers, the families and most of all the children.

Self-Awareness begins through self-reflection. It helps you understand yourself and become more objective and thoughtful about your relationships with children and the way you approach teaching. You need to take the time to step outside of your experiences and reflect on them. It begins with you – your "self". In order to lead and inspire children we must be in touch with ourselves. When you raise your own awareness, you are able to understand others' perspectives and values. The goal is to understand another individual's point of view. We view our life through our own lens of values and beliefs. As you raise your self-awareness, you learn to put aside your own lens, you are less judgmental, and are able to detach emotionally from the situation. Knowing how you operate and how to adjust your behavior in a professional manner is the key to being a strong leader.

Being self-aware is an on-going process. You don't graduate with a diploma: it is a daily task of monitoring your behaviors. Sometimes you fall back into your old patterns, it happens. Remember, there are no mistakes, only learning experiences. Each experience will provide the opportunity to reflect, be mindful and respond appropriately. Maya Angelou said it best, "when you know better, you do better." And when you know better you teach from a place of knowledge, not from opinions.

What exactly is gossip?

According to the Cambridge English dictionary, gossip is conversation or reports about other people's private lives that may be untrue and unkind. Gossiping or spreading rumors is not limited to verbal conversation, it includes emailing and texting. Gossiping is stating something about another that you would not say directly to that person. Often gossiping about another individual behind their back causes a bond between those engaged in the gossip. As you become more self-aware, gossip feels uncomfortable. You learn to respect and honor all your co-workers, those present and those not present. You disengage from any source of conversation that is hurtful to another human being. Remember children are like sponges; they absorb what they hear as truth and will often repeat verbatim what they hear. There is no room for gossip in the workplace, and certainly not in the classroom.

Gossip in the work environment is a major cause of conflict and disruption. It spreads like cancer. It is toxic. It is negative. It is hurtful. All it takes is two people to cause an out of control wildfire.

A practical guide to live by is Don Miquel Ruiz's "Four Agreements."

1. **Be impeccable with your word** - speak with integrity. Say only what you mean. Avoid using the word to speak against yourself or to gossip about others. Use the power of your word in the direction of truth and love.

2. **Don't take anything personally** - nothing others do is because of you. What others say and do is a projection of their own reality, their own dream. When you are immune to the opinions and actions of others, you won't be the victim of needless suffering.

3. **Don't make assumptions** - find the courage to ask questions and to express what you really want. Communicate with others as clearly as you can to avoid misunderstandings, sadness, and drama. With just this one agreement, you completely transform your life.

4. **Always do your best -** your best is going to change from moment to moment; it will be different when you are healthy as opposed to sick. Under any circumstance, simply do your best and you will avoid self-judgment, self-abuse and regret.

Responding vs. Reacting

How do you respond to conflict in general, but more precisely, in your classroom? It has been said that 10% of your life experience is dependent on what happens to you and 90% is based on how you respond. This statement emphasizes the importance of how we respond when faced with conflicts, problems or challenging behaviors.

Examine your reactions when a child is presenting a challenging behavior. Do you respond in ways that are effective, constructive, and teach a skill, or do you react with emotions? It is not about controlling the behaviors, it is about connection; the only behavior you can control is your own. When you make the connection, you do not need control. I will discuss this in more detail in another chapter.

Examine reasons for reacting with emotions:

- A child has pushed your buttons.

- You don't feel in control of the situation which brings on feelings of incompetency and inadequacy.

- You are taking the child's behavior personally.

- You are feeling the behavior is a reflection of who you are, or how you teach, or how you manage a classroom.

The first step is to manage your own behavior. Challenging behaviors are just that, challenging. They are the trigger to our own emotions, judgements and beliefs. They require a great deal of effort on your part. Calm starts with YOU. You are the adult. You are the emotional regulator, the barometer. Quiet the chatter in your head so you can be present for the child. When you are calm the children will feel that calmness and model that same emotion. They learn the skill of calming down from you. Both child and adult need to be in a state of calmness in order for learning and reasoning to take place.

Understanding child development will help you be more patient, and patience will help you remain calm, thus, allowing you to model with encouragement, and not with punishment. Yet there are times when you will feel frustrated, maybe multiple times in a day. Knowing and understanding your own triggers will help you develop your coping mechanisms. Learn to recognize when you need a time out or a moment of reflection to utilize your own self-calming techniques. Learn to shift from control to connection, from confrontations to conversations. Have realistic expectations for all concerned. And most of all, be the change you want to see.

It is important to have strategies to build immunity against burnout, strategies for calming the body and the mind. Teachers get upset, too, and need to have calming techniques for themselves.

Calming techniques:

- Practice mindfulness and become aware of your feelings.

- Journal every day in detail. Journaling promotes awareness and helps to release frustrations in order not to bring them into the classroom. Write your feelings, your thoughts, the highs and lows of your day; notice any patterns, maybe some defeating ones.

- Keep a daily gratitude list. It will help you stay focused on the positive things in your life.

Calming techniques while in the midst of the storm:

- Take a break from the room whenever possible.

- Breathe deeply.

- Count backwards from twenty.

Once you are calm you can teach the children how to calm themselves. A simple calming technique for children can be taught during circle time, when there is quiet and not crisis.

Calming techniques for children:

Pizza Breath: Hold your hands out flat in front of you and make your hands into a shape of a pizza.

- Take a deep breath in - smell the pizza.

- Count to three and hold in the breath.

- Blow out the breath - the pizza is hot.

Do this 3-5 times. Teach this prior to problems.

Calm Down Center: The calm down center is a safe place in the classroom for the children to gain control of their emotions. It can consist of two comfy chairs or bean bag chairs, or even a few large, soft pillows. Include the "calm-down-caddy" (see below). Display a large colorful poster at the child's eye level demonstrating the visual steps for "pizza breathing," and the problem-solving steps to help provide directions on how the child can calm down. The calm down center, or cooling down time, is different from time out. In the calm down center the child is not alone, the teacher stays in the same proximity, while in time out, the child is alone. The goal is for the child to learn from their mistakes, rather than punishing them. Sometimes the only way a teacher can help a child to calm down is by separating them from the situation. Once everyone is calm, the teacher can problem solve, which will be discussed later.

Counting to Ten: The teacher stands in front of the class and raises her arms high above her head and asks the children to do the same. The teacher slowly counts to ten; as she is counting she lowers her arms down alongside her body. The children follow along with the teacher. The teacher can also incorporate deep inhales and exhales as the arms lift and lower.

Calm Down Caddy: The caddy consists of an assortment of crayons, paper, playdough, squishes, markers, puppets, anything to occupy the child to help them return to being calm. The children can also take part in putting the caddy together.

Raggedy Ann/Robot: Ask the children to stand stiff like a robot and then quickly go limp like a ragdoll. They can stand stiff like the robot on an inhalation and go limp on the exhalation. This can be repeated several times.

The Child's Pose: The child's pose is a yoga pose for relaxing. Ask the children to kneel down on all fours, then sit back on their heels (buttocks over heels). They can create a pillow with their hands (one hand on top of the other) with their forehead resting on their hands, or they can place their hands alongside their body. The teacher tells the children to breathe deeply and rest. Soft music playing in the background is helpful.

We are always evolving and learning every day. It is the process not the end product. Choose to be open to understand yourself, and this will give you the ability to understand others. Throughout the day whenever possible, sit a moment and enjoy the children at play. Observe your interactions and connections with the children. Your powerful interactions with the children will make a difference for them NOW and in the FUTURE.

Exercise:

Through self-reflection you have the opportunity to raise your consciousness. Review the questions below and do your best to answer them honestly.

Self-Reflection classroom questions:

- Can I be fully present for the children?

- Do I partake in gossip?

- Do I practice calming techniques?

- How do I respond to conflicts?

- What is it that I do best?

- What do I value and what is important to me?

- What can I do to improve my life?

- What motivates me?

- What are my thinking patterns/internal thoughts?

- What situations/triggers make me react?

- Am I aware of my body language, tone of voice, language expression?

- Am I aware of my own feelings?

- Am I able to manage my emotions?

- Do I know my level of frustration?

- Observe – am I reacting or responding?

- Do I have a sense of empathy?

Ingredient #2: Richly Rooted in Knowledge

"Education is the most powerful weapon which you can use to change the world."

Nelson Mandela

Knowledge of Brain Development

Long before birth the brain is building neural connections (pathways) that will be responsible for everything from breathing, and sight, to abilities to speak, think and reason.

Although the brain is developed during pregnancy, it is not fully formed and operational at birth. The early development provides the necessary brain function to keep the baby alive. The brain has not reached its full growth of maturation which depends on the exposure to various experiences obtained from the environment and from relationships. The brain develops physiologically in response to experiences throughout childhood. With each experience, the brain of a child age birth to three builds trillions of new connections. Most of the growth happens during the first three years of life. (Zero to Three). By age five 90% of the child's brain is developed. (Harvard Center for the Developing Child). The environment influences how these connections form. The number of connections can go up or go down, depending on the enrichment of the environment. At this time the brain is the most flexible and prepared to learn (Plasticity). Early childhood experiences physically determine how the brain is "wired." The brain grows as a result of continued exposure to experiences. Learning can actually alter the physical structure of the brain. Each time a new skill is learned the brain connection, or synapse, is formed. Connections are made permanent from early infancy to early childhood. However, the brain is influenced during pregnancy by the overall health of the mother, her stress levels, and the use of alcohol and drugs.

During the first three years a child's brain is making an abundance of connections which form a huge number of synapses, but not every synapse will be used. Therefore, the brain "prunes" or eliminates the unused synapses of the brain. This process of pruning or eliminating the unused synapses ensures the brain will function more efficiently.

Children in their first three years have the capacity to learn language, even more than one language, due to the brain's circuitry system that enables the child to comprehend and reproduce what they hear. Babies develop the ability to talk by hearing what is said to them.

The first three years are important for laying the groundwork for heathy development (Center for Early education and Development 2001). Although the brain connector's density is at its highest level in the first three years, learning continues well beyond this time.

Neuroscientists are finding that a strong, secure attachment to a nurturing caregiver can have a protective biological function in helping a growing child withstand the ordinary stresses of daily life (Shore, 1997). This attachment, including consistent care, teaches the baby trust and creates a sense of emotional security. When a child is adopted into a family system, the adoptive parents create the experience of a secure attachment. If the mother or the caregiver does not respond to an infant's needs, and does not bond with the child from birth, the lack of nurturing can cause delays in developing trust and the child may not be ready to move toward autonomy.

A child born to a mother who has used and abused alcohol and drugs is at high risk for cognitive and emotional delays with a lack of vital sensory input, (not speaking to the infant, not making eye contact, not stroking the child), the brain's circuitry becomes impaired, making it is difficult for the child to process sights, sounds and sensation. For brain growth to occur a child needs to be held and spoken to. Even a very young infant learns the meaning of behavior by watching the mother's facial expressions, hearing the tone of her voice, and feeling safe in her arms. The child that is neglected is prone to delayed learning, suffers from the inability to attach or to be touched, and has problems coping with noisy places and changes in plans.

When a child's mind is overwhelmed with stress, either by their home environment or classroom environment, the emotions negatively affect brain functioning. Sensing danger, the amygdala (the brain structure that processes experiences into emotions) sends out strong stress hormones to the hippocampus. Part of the amygdala's job is to quickly process and express emotions, especially fear and anger. This primitive part of the brain responds in flight, fight, or freeze. The stress hormones actually cause damage to the dendrites of the hippocampus. Healthy communication between the hippocampus and other parts of the brain, including those that mediate thoughts, is then disrupted (LeDoux, 1996). Therefore, when the child's brain is under stress it is difficult for learning to take place. Early interventions can make a difference in the child's development.

Enhancing Brain Development in the Classroom

It is common knowledge that a well-balanced diet, sufficient sleep and plenty of exercise support healthy brain growth and have a positive effect on learning. Children are active and movement stimulates connections in the brain. Daily exercise and time outdoors are essential for health and well-being. Early childhood educators can help develop these synapses by constantly providing new experiences to stimulate the child's brain. Repetition of the experiences strengthens the synapse. Children are active and willing learners. They learn by using their five senses. The more their senses are involved, by feeling, tasting, smelling, hearing and seeing, the more information is absorbed and the more skills can be learned.

Infants: It is important for a baby to bond with their caregiver/teacher to develop trust with the person they will spend many hours a day. When an infant feels safe and secure, learning can take place. Children do not need special toys or videos to stimulate their brain development and support synapse growth. Stimulation can take place while changing the infant's diaper, by talking, singing, positive eye contact, letting the child hold onto a toy to explore what it is, and by "floor time" where the child can explore objects and physical space.

Toddlers: Toddlers are at the stage of using words to express their feelings, they are learning how to act appropriately in situations and how to take turns and share.

When a child is in the midst of a meltdown, it may elicit very strong emotions for early educators, but this behavior is normal development. The meltdown begins in the child's brain.

The brain has two sides: the right side of the brain uses feelings, symbols, and images, while the left side uses logic, reasoning, order and language. At the toddler age the child's right side is more developed than the left, which means the toddler will exhibit more feelings than reason about a situation. In the child's mind this is a true crisis. When a child erupts in anger because there is no more yellow paint, the primitive part of the brain has received an intense surge of energy, leaving the child literally unable to act calmly and reasonably. No matter how many times you tell the child that he has plenty of blue paint, he is probably not going to listen to reason in this moment. He is much more likely to throw something or yell.

It is best at this time for the early educator to soothe the child by acknowledging his feelings of anger and frustration and shift his attention. When the educator understands that learning changes the physical structure of the brain, they are more able to prevent the child's outburst of emotions.

Preschool: Early childhood educators can create and maintain an environment of encouragement and respect, by giving the child choices and allowing the child the opportunity to take the initiative.

Children need many different opportunities to practice new skills and take initiative. Children need to explore concepts over time which allows them to make connections. For a connection to become permanent, it must be practiced and used repeatedly which gives a greater chance for the information to move from the working memory to the long-term memory.

Emotions play a significant role in learning. In order for children to learn, they need to feel safe and confident. Stress on the other hand can destroy brain cells and make learning more difficult. Secure relationships with family, teachers and other significant people are essential to a child's learning. The brains of children develop best in enriched environments (Diamond & Hopson, 1998). It is the early educator's role to connect to each child, to build trust, to provide appropriate choices, and to allow the child to explore and encourage questions.

How a teacher treats a child is as important as what they teach. A successful educator will possess a solid understanding of brain development, be able to respond to behaviors with compassion, use a soft touch on the shoulder, a calm voice, eye contact and validate a child's feelings. In doing so, the educator will be able to disengage the child's amygdala so the child can be calmed down and be able to respond with redirection or problem solving.

Exercise:

1. What are ways that you can build the synapse connections in an infant, toddler and preschooler?
2. Identify different activities that stimulate a child's brain development.

Knowledge of Child Development

Child development encompasses the biological, psychological and emotional changes that all children experience as they progress from birth to adolescence and move forward from the dependent stage to autonomy. All children go through the same stages of development in sequential order, but at their own time.

When there are changes in a child's development they are referred to as developmental milestones.

A child's development also depends on their parents and the quality of care that was provided during the growing years. Parents, caregivers, teachers, child care centers and the preschool environment play an important role in the child's development that is essential to living in society. For this reason, all those involved in a child's development need to fully understand the social, cognitive, emotional and educational needs of children. Extended research in this field has resulted in new speculations and tactics. Understanding the roots of researched theories for child development is necessary for executing developmentally appropriate practices in the classroom.

Jean Piaget- 1896-1980 Cognitive Development

Piaget's theory describes the cognitive development in children. His concepts have become the foundation for developmentally appropriate practices and curricula. Based on his observations children think differently than adults. Piaget suggested that intelligence develops through a series of four stages. All children will go through the four stages, but at their own rate. His findings were that children understand the world by manipulating concrete objects in their environment.

A child's knowledge develops as they make discoveries and incorporate their new insights. Schemas are continually modified by the processes that Piaget termed assimilation and accommodation.

- Schemas: Categories of knowledge that help a child understand.
- Assimilation: The process of incorporating new experiences into existing schema's (child sees a zebra and based on its appearance calls it a horse).
- Accommodation: What happens when the schema itself changes to accommodate the new knowledge. New information changes what we already know (the child learns that the horse with stripes is a different animal called a zebra).

Piaget's Four Stages of Cognitive Development

1. Sensorimotor Stage: (birth -2 years old)

During this stage infants and toddlers learn through manipulating objects and through sensory experiences (touch, taste, hearing, sight, and smell); they learn through the actions of sucking, grasping, looking and listening. The more the child interacts within their environment, the more they discover about the world around them. Children have significant physical/mental/emotional growth at this stage.

During the last part of the sensorimotor stage Piaget believed that object permanence is developing. Object Permanence is the understanding that things will continue to exist even though they cannot be seen. Children are learning that they are separate beings from the people and objects around them. They are beginning to assign words to objects.

2. Preoperational Stage: (2-7 years old)

Children start to think symbolically and begin to learn to use words and pictures to represent objects in their environment. There is an emergence in their language and thinking skills. Children learn through play, although they are still egocentric thinking in concrete terms. It is difficult for them to see other's perspectives and points of view.

Because a child's thinking is emerging, they think differently than adults do. They do not understand the concept of conservation, how the same portion of a material when in two different forms is still the same amount.

For example, a teacher can take a lump of clay and divide it into two equal pieces. One piece of clay is rolled into a ball while the other is flattened into a pancake shape. When the preoperational child is asked which piece of clay is bigger, they choose the piece that is flat and spread out, because it appears bigger. Another example is two cups, one is tall and the other is short. Eight ounces of water is poured into each cup, and the child is asked which one of the cups has more water in it, which one has less. The child will answer the tall cup has more and the short cup has less. As adults we understand it is the same amount of water, but the child who has not yet entered the concrete-operational development stage is not able to identify that each cup holds the same amount of water.

3. Concrete Operational Stage: (7-11 years old)

During this stage children begin to think logically about concrete events and the concept of conservation. Their thinking becomes more logical and organized. Egocentrism of the

Preoperational Stage starts to diminish and children have a better understanding of other's points of view and learn that not everyone shares their same perspective. Abstract problem solving can be possible, although some children are still inclined to struggle with abstract concepts.

4. Formal Operational Thought: (11-15 years old)

At this stage children are starting to think logically and organized and are using conceptual reasoning. A child can think logically about a problem. They also begin to think abstractly.

Understanding Piaget's Theory in the Early Childhood Classroom

The teacher's main role is the facilitation of learning by providing various experiences for the students. "Discovery Learning" allows opportunities for students to explore and experiment, while encouraging new understandings. Opportunities that allow learners of different cognitive levels to work together often help encourage less mature students to advance to a higher understanding of the material. (Wood, 2008) For the purpose of this book applying Piaget's theory in the early childhood classroom, we are going to focus on the Sensorimotor Stage and Preoperational Stage.

Sensorimotor Stage: Learning about their world through their five senses and the lack of language.

At this stage there needs to be several one-on-one meaningful interactions with the appropriate materials in order for the child to experience and explore with their five senses, which provides a rich stimulating classroom.

Preoperational Stage: The child is egocentric and doesn't have the ability to understand another's point of view. As per (Slavin, 2005) there are four main teaching implications drawn from Piaget's theory:

1. Focus on the process of children's thinking, not just its products.
2. Recognition of the crucial role of children's self-initiated, active involvement in learning activities. In a Piagetian classroom, children are encouraged to discover themselves through spontaneous interaction with the environment, rather than the presentation of ready-made knowledge.
3. A de-emphasize on practice aimed at making children adult-like in their thinking. Piaget believed trying to speed up a child's process through the stages could be worse than no teaching at all.
4. Acceptance of individual differences in developmental progress. Piaget's theory asserts that children go through all the same developmental stages, however, they do so at different rates. Teachers must make a special effort to arrange classroom activities for individuals and groups of children rather than for the whole class group. Small Groups!

The <u>University of Arkansas</u> suggests six steps to structure preoperational development:

1. Use concrete props and visual aids whenever possible.

2. Make instructions relatively short, using actions as well as words.

3. Do not expect the students to consistently see the world from someone else's point of view.

4. Be sensitive to the possibility that students may have different meanings for the same word or different words for the same meaning. Students may also expect everyone to understand words they have invented.

5. Give children a great deal of hands-on practice with the skills that serve as building blocks for more complex skills like reading comprehension.

6. Provide a wide range of experiences in order to build a foundation for concept learning and language.

Erik Erickson 1902-1994   Psychosocial Theory of Personality Development

Erik Erikson's theory is known as the psychosocial theory of personality development. Erikson placed a great deal of importance to the social environment in a person's psychological development. Erikson believed every person passes through eight stages in their life span.

Eight Stages of Man:

- Trust vs. Mistrust - (birth to 18 months)
- Autonomy vs. Shame & Doubt - (2-4 years)
- Initiative vs. Guilt - (3-5 years)
- Industry vs. Inferiority - (6-12 years)
- Identity vs. Role Confusion - (12-18 years)
- Intimacy vs. Isolation - (young adulthood)
- Generativity vs. Self-Absorption - (middle adulthood)
- Integrity vs. Despair - (late adulthood**)**

At each stage there is a sequence of conflicts that children or adults face a need to be balanced for healthy development to take place and move into the next sequential stage. If balance is not attained, Erickson predicted that a child or an adult would have ongoing problems related to that stage. As an example, during the first stage of "Trust vs. Mistrust," if the quality of care is healthy in infancy and the caregiver consistently meets the needs of the infant, the child learns to trust the world to meet their needs. If, however, the quality of care was not healthy, trust remains an unresolved issue throughout the stages of development. For the purpose of this book we are going to focus on the first three stages.

0-1 year	Trust vs. Mistrust
2-3 years	Autonomy vs. Shame/Doubt
4-5 years	Initiative vs. Guilt

Stage 1: Trust vs. Mistrust (Birth-2 years of age)

Trust comes from the caregiver providing consistently in meeting the needs of the infant. When an infant's needs are met, the infant will gain a basic sense of trust in the world, a world that is safe, reliable and responsive to their needs. Providing a sense of trust helps the child accept limits and boundaries. Caregivers who do not respond to an infant's cry from hunger and who do not provide comfort, will contribute to the infant developing a sense of mistrust.

Stage 2: Autonomy vs. Shame (2-4 years old)

This stage is commonly referred to as the *terrible twos* which is acting with will and control. The children in this stage are beginning to explore their environment and gain an expression of autonomy or independence which is built on the trust stage. If a child's independence is prevented the child develops a sense of shame and this prevents the healthy acceptance of limits and boundaries. A child develops a sense of independence when the adults in their lives allow them the chance to do things on their own. When the adults criticize the child on their tasks it diminishes the child's effort and they may develop shame and doubt.

Stage 3: Initiative vs. Guilt (4-6 years old)

The child in this stage is beginning to develop their relationships with peers, make their own decisions, and have the initiative to carry them out primarily through their play. The child takes pride in their accomplishments and responsibilities. There is a high emphasis on experimenting, exploring and pursuing their own interest in an effort to balance the initiative vs guilt. A child with initiative is excited to try out new materials and concepts. Discouraging initiative can produce guilt.

Understanding Erik Erickson's Theory in an Early Childhood Classroom

Teachers who understand how to apply psychosocial development in the classroom create a safe environment where the child is free to explore and learn new knowledge.

Trust vs. Mistrust - the infant caregiver/teachers must respond to the infant's individual needs, provide comfort, boundaries, and sensory stimulating objects to manipulate.

Autonomy vs. Shame - at this stage the teachers need to allow the child to explore by using their senses, providing plenty of play for social interaction, implementing child directed activities where the child can choose their activity, and encouraging responsibilities, such as classroom jobs to help develop their independence.

Initiative vs. Guilt - the teacher will need to provide plenty of room for imaginative play and expression. Reading stories and singing songs will enhance and stimulate their imagination.

Create projects that are based on the child's interest, let children pick their own books to read, breakdown all tasks into simple steps to avoid them becoming overwhelmed and frustrated. Teachers will need to provide continuous encouragement and feedback, offer choices with limits, ask open ended questions, and when a child makes a poor choice, show them how to solve the problem.

Abraham Maslow: 1908- 1970 Basic Needs and Learning

Maslow was a humanist psychologist who developed a hierarchy pyramid of needs in which he theorized that basic needs for humans must be met before they can reach their full potential. In order for children to focus and learn the hierarchy, their basic needs must be met. This theory can directly affect a child's ability to learn. If all these needs are met, self-actualization can be achieved.

The basic needs are:
- Physiological
- Safety
- Love and Belonging
- Self-Esteem
- Self-Actualization

Physiological needs are food, water and sleep. These needs must be met because a child who is hungry, tired or thirsty has difficulty focusing, therefore, cannot learn.

Safety is a security from danger. When children know they are safe and protected they feel free to explore their environment. Children with disabilities may need extra attention to feel safe and secure.

Love & Belonging is the sense of being connected to others as a result of receiving acceptance, respect, and love. When a child feels connected or that they belong, it promotes their learning. Feeling connected for some children may not be an easy task, as they may feel they are not worthy of love. As a result, they may exhibit negative acting out behavior that tests their acceptance. These children benefit from being around adults who are consistent and caring, not harsh and judgmental.

Self-Esteem emerges from daily experiences. If children's experiences are mainly positive, their sense of self grows. A supportive environment encourages children to view themselves as individuals who are capable of achieving accomplishments. When a child's experiences are predominantly positive, the sense of self develops.

Self-Actualization is achieving one's fullest potential.

Understanding Abraham Maslow's Theory in an Early Childhood Classroom

Teachers must be cognizant of every child's needs. When physical security and safety, including sleep, are challenged, students will use most of their time, energy, and creativity simply trying to survive. This struggle interferes with learning. The teacher must create a safe environment by providing a structured predictable classroom where the children can take risks and not be ridiculed or teased. Providing predictable structure removes the fear of the unknown. It is also necessary for teachers to constantly be aware of their own body language, tone of voice, and the language they use. A warm welcome to each child by using the child's name can promote a feeling of belonging. Smiling at the children, having fun with "high fives," offering specific encouragement, and problem solving with other children can develop a sense of belonging. Children need to know they are a welcomed and feel they are part of the class.

Lev Vygotsky: 1896-1934 Social Interaction and Learning

Vygotsky focuses on social interaction in the development of cognition. Vygotsky theorized that children not only learn by manipulating objects, but also through interactions with adults and more experienced peers. He believed pretend play is the most important vehicle for children ages 2-5 years of age.

The two theories Vygotsky developed are:

Scaffolding: is a temporary platform erected during the building or repair of a building. The scaffolding is removed when the project is completed. In Vygotsky's view of cognitive development, adults serve a similar purpose of scaffolding, they help and support a child while learning new information and developing more complex thinking abilities.

The Zone of Proximal Development: is the space between a child being able to do an activity on his own or with some scaffolding or help from the outside. His theory is the activity that children couldn't complete on their own could be accomplished with help from another person more cognitively advanced than themselves (Hung & Nichani, 2002).

Understanding Lev Vygotsky's Theory in an Early Childhood Classroom

When teachers implement Vygotsky's theory into an early childhood classroom, they need to provide verbal directions, physical assistance, and ask questions to help children improve skills and acquire knowledge. Teachers can also guide those peers who have advanced skills to help other children grow and learn by modeling or providing verbal guidance. The teacher is constantly providing support to the child until the child can complete the task independently.

However, there are times when the teacher will need to redirect the child in order for the child to succeed. Such as the child who is not capable of placing the correct puzzle pieces into the puzzle, regardless of how much scaffolding the teacher provides. In a situation like this it is apparent the child has gone beyond his ZPD (Zone of Proximal Development) and this particular puzzle is too advanced for this child. In a case like this the teacher will need to remove that puzzle and replace it with another that can challenge the child but also be one the child will be able to complete.

The opposite example is the child who masters a ten-piece puzzle in less than a minute. This child falls outside the ZPD and needs a more challenging puzzle, either with more pieces or more complex shapes or designs.

In both of these examples, the Vygotsky teacher needs to be alert to each child's capabilities and provide the appropriate task to meet the child's level of skill in order to assist in their cognitive development.

Howard Gardner 1943 Multiple Intelligences

Gardner founded the theory of multiple intelligences. Gardner stated that a person's intelligence is multifaceted and that people can be intelligent in many different ways: not everyone is able to learn in the same uniform way. His theory has identified eight multiple intelligences.

Eight Intelligences:

1. Linguistic- Word Smart
2. Logical/Mathematical- Logic Smart
3. Musical/Rhythmic- Music Smart
4. Bodily/Kinesthetic- Body Smart
5. Spatial/Visual- Picture Smart
6. Naturalist- Nature Smart
7. Intrapersonal- People Smart
8. Interpersonal –Self Smart

Linguistic: They can be taught by encouraging them to say and see words, read books together. Tools include computers, games, multimedia, books, tape recorders, and lecture.

Logical/Mathematical: They think conceptually, abstractly, and are able to see and explore patterns and relationships. They like to experiment, solve puzzles, ask cosmic questions. They can be taught through logic games, investigations, mysteries. They need to learn and form concepts before they can deal with details.

Musical: They love music, but they are also sensitive to sounds in their environments. They may study better with music in the background. They can be taught by turning lessons into lyrics, speaking rhythmically, tapping out time. Tools include musical instruments, music, radio, stereo, CD-ROM, multimedia.

Bodily/Kinesthetic: They like movement, making things, touching. They communicate well through body language and can be taught through physical activity, hands-on learning, acting out, role playing. Tools include equipment and real objects.

Spatial/Visual: They are very aware of their environments. They like to draw, do jigsaw puzzles, read maps, daydream. They can be taught through drawings, verbal and physical imagery. Tools include models, graphics, charts, photographs, drawings, 3-D modeling, video, videoconferencing, television, multimedia, texts with pictures/charts/graphs.

Naturalistic Intelligence: These learners have the ability to see patterns in nature. Because they love and understand plants, animals and nature, they can learn by using examples of nature.

Intrapersonal: These learners tend to shy away from others. They're in tune with their inner feelings; they have wisdom, intuition and motivation, as well as a strong will, confidence and opinions. They can be taught through independent study and introspection. Tools include books, creative materials, diaries, privacy and time. They are the most independent of the learners.

Interpersonal: These students learn through interaction. They have many friends, empathy for others, street smarts. They can be taught through group activities, seminars, dialogues. Tools include the telephone, audio conferencing, time and attention from the instructor, video conferencing, writing, computer conferencing, e-mail.

Understanding Howard Gardner's Theory in an Early Childhood Classroom

This approach provides a framework to identify how children learn; to build on their strongest assets; to help them become more intelligent by exposing them to a variety of ways of learning; to better individualize for their interests and needs; and to use teaching strategies that make learning more efficient, successful, and enjoyable for all children. We can foster meaningful learning experiences by using multiple teaching tools and strategies and by building positive, supportive relationships with children. Through environments that offer a variety of stimulating, hands-on materials that children individually select, and by creating learning centers that provide natural opportunities to move, be active, and fully engaged in either solo or small group experiences, we better serve and meet the needs of more children.

Linguistic/Verbal Intelligence: Children who are strong in this area may like to play with words and the sounds of language, are good at telling stories, love looking at and hearing books read, and experiment with writing.

The following items can be provided in the classroom to increase their strengths and align with their linguistic/verbal learning style.

- Story time
- Flannel boards
- Library
- Writing center
- Listening center

Logical/ Mathematical Intelligence: Children who show talent in this area may like to reason and solve problems, explore patterns and categorize objects, ask questions and experiment, and count and understand one-to-one correspondence.

The following items can be provided in the classroom to increase their strengths and align with their logical/math learning style.

- Puzzles
- Computer
- Cooking
- Math center
- Science center

Musical/Rhythmic Intelligence: Children with this intelligence may sing, hum, or whistle to themselves, see patterns in music and nature, be sensitive to environmental sounds and the human voice, and respond to music emotionally.

The following items can be provided in the classroom to increase their strengths and align with their musical learning style.

- Instruments
- Singing
- Listening center
- Music

Spatial/Visual Intelligence: Children who are strong in this area may think in images, know where everything in the classroom is located, be fascinated with the way things work, and take toys apart to see how they work.

The following items can be provided in the classroom to increase their strengths and align with their visual/spatial learning style.

- Manipulatives
- Puzzles
- Blocks
- Media center
- Computer center
- Art Center

Naturalistic Intelligence: Children who are strong in this area may observe nature, notice changes in the environment, enjoy conducting experiments, sort and categorize objects, like using magnifying glasses, microscopes, binoculars and telescopes to study nature, like to care for pets, and enjoy gardening.

The following items can be provided in the classroom to increase their strengths and align with their naturalistic learning style.

- Science center
- Nature walks
- Plants

Bodily/Kinesthetic Intelligence: Children with talent in this area may have good fine motor skills and coordination, learn by moving, not by sitting still, feel things in their "gut", be athletic or good dancers; and physically mimic others.

The following items can be provided in the classroom to increase their strengths and align with their kinesthetic learning style.

- Dance
- Woodworking center

- Manipulative center
- Imaginative-play center
- Playground/outdoor play
- Tactile-learning center

Interpersonal Intelligence: Children who are strong in this area may have several "best friends", be good at resolving conflict, be leaders and group organizers, and "read" other peoples' feelings and behavior accurately.

The following items can be provided in the classroom to increase their strengths and align with their interpersonal learning style.

- Puppet theater
- Dramatic play center
- Group discussion
- Conflict Resolution area

Intrapersonal Intelligence: Children with this intelligence may be aware of their emotions, express their feelings well, require private space and time, and have realistic knowledge of their own strengths and challenges.

The following items can be provided in the classroom to increase their strengths and align with their intrapersonal learning style.

- One-person activities
- Life skills/self-help activities

- Computer center (e.g., self-paced software)

Sara Smilansky's 1922-2006 Children Learn Through Play

Sara Smilansky is a psychologist known for her four stages of play. These play stages are considered to reflect a child's cognitive development. Her research demonstrated how the relationship of academic success is based on a child's play.

Four stages of play:

- Functional
- Constructive
- Symbolic/pretend
- Games with Rules

1. **Functional play:** The first type of play that follows through to early childhood as new objects are introduced. During this exploratory play a child uses their senses to experiment with different objects in their environment, while repeating their actions over and over.

2. **Constructive play:** This stage begins from the middle to late toddler. In constructive play children learn the different uses of play materials, and they base their play on a plan and a goal. At this stage children have a longer attention span than that of a child in the functional play stage.

3. **Symbolic play:** A pretend play that is open ended. Pretend Play can develop alongside constructive play. When two or more children are playing it is considered socio-dramatic play.

4. **Games with rules:** In this type of play children follow a set of rules and work toward a common goal. Games with rules involve planning. This stage needs children to demonstrate self-control to follow the rules.

Understanding Sara Smilansky's Play Theory in an Early Childhood Classroom

Play enhances children's creativity, problem solving skills, and helps to develop self-regulation, taking turns, and following rules. During symbolic play children start to learn to consider other's perspectives. Smilansky's theory applied in an early childhood classroom would have lots of child directed play! So play, play, play!!! Play is a child's work.

Infants engage in solitary-functional play; therefore, the teacher needs to provide sensory activities by continually introducing new objects and materials for the infant to manipulate. Infants enjoy playing with their new objects over and over. Toddlers on the other hand, engage in parallel-functional play, which means that toddlers play alongside other children. Offering a variety of multiple sensory materials when interacting with the child, the teacher can play with a goal in mind. Preschoolers engage in pretend play and need an assortment of pretend objects for them to manipulate and help to stimulate creative imaginations. At the four and five-year old stage, children are engaging in cooperative constructive play, socio-dramatic play, and are beginning to start to have the self-control to learn games with rules.

The teacher will need to encourage play in the classroom and introduce some games with rules which can help children solve their problems.

John Bowlby's 1907-1990 & Ann Ainsworth's 1913-1999 Attachment Theory

Bowlby's & Anisworth's studies found strong attachment to a caregiver provides a necessary sense of security and foundation, especially at the infant/toddler stage. The secure attachment allows the child to explore and develop. Without such a relationship in place, Bowlby found that a great deal of developmental energy is expended in the search for stability and security.

Types of Attachment:

- **Secure Attachment:** When the caregiver is present the child will play within a strange setting. They are calmed by the caregiver's proximity, may cry when the caregiver leaves, but will be happy when caregiver returns.

- **Avoidant Attachment:** The child in general is not distressed when the caregiver leaves the room and may ignore or not acknowledge when the caregiver returns.

- **Ambivalent Attachment:** The child is usually distressed when their caregiver leaves the room and can be inconsolable when the caregiver returns and attempts to calm them.

- **Disorganized Attachment:** The child has no consistent pattern of responses when their caregiver leaves or returns.

Understanding John Bowlby's Attachment Theory in an Early Childhood Classroom

The ways in which a teacher can attach and build the trust with a child is by meeting their needs, responding to their cries, interacting, playing, eye contact, appropriate touching, talking and singing to the child and allowing them to explore the environment. Each time a child is held, rocked, fed, and spoken to, these interactions will assist in developing a secure attachment.

The more consistent and longevity of a teacher, the more likely the child will develop a secure relationship and the secondary attachment will be enhanced.

Alexander Thomas (1914-2003) & Stella Chess (1914-2007)

Alexander Thomas and Stella Chess were infant researchers that identified three basic types of temperaments that many people in the field call "Easy/Flexible," "Slow to Warm/Fearful," and "Difficult/Feisty." How an adult relates to the child's temperament can play a big role in the child's emotional wellbeing. Any temperament trait can be an asset or a liability to a child's development, depending on whether the adults recognize what type of approach is best suited to that child.

Temperaments

Infants, right from birth, are all different in the way they respond to the world. Each has his or her own way of showing feelings and responding to the world around him or her (Chess). According to Dr. Stella Chase, the differences are visible in the first few months of life, such as how active the child is, whether the child has a regular or irregular sleep pattern, how the child accepts new people or new foods, how long does it take for the child to adjust to their environment, the child's moods, how sensitive is the child to texture, sights and sounds. These traits make up a child's individual temperament.

Three Temperament Types (California Education & West Ed, 2011)

1. **The Easy or Flexible Child** (About 40% of most groups of children). Typically, the easy child is regular in biological rhythms, optimistically approaches most new situations, adapts quickly, and has a predominantly positive mood of low or medium intensity. Such a child is indeed easy for the caregiver. She or he is easily toilet trained, learns to sleep through the night, has regular feedings and nap routines, takes to most new situations and people pleasantly, usually adapts to change quickly, is generally cheerful, and expresses her or his distress or frustration mildly. In fact, children with easy temperaments may show very deep feelings with only a single tear rolling down a cheek.

2. **The Difficult or Feisty Child** (About 10% of children). The difficult child is the opposite of the easy child. The child may be not sleep through the night, her or his feeding and nap schedules may change from day to day, and the child may be difficult to toilet train because of irregular bowel movements. The difficult child typically fusses or even cries loudly at anything new and usually adapts slowly. All too often this type of child expresses an unpleasant or disagreeable mood and, if frustrated, may even have a temper tantrum. In contrast to the "easy" child's reaction, an intense, noisy reaction by the difficult child may not signify a depth of feeling. Often the best way to handle such outbursts is just to wait them out. Caregivers who do not understand this type of temperament as normal sometimes feel resentment at the child for being so difficult to manage. They may scold, pressure, or appease the child, which only reinforces the difficult temperament and is likely to result in a true behavior problem. Understanding,

patience, and consistency, on the other hand, will lead to a "goodness of fit," with a final positive adjustment to life's demands.

3. **The Slow-to-Warm-Up or Fearful Child** (About 15% of children). Finally, there is a group of children who are often called shy. The child in this group also has discomfort with anything new and adapts slowly; but unlike the difficult child, this child's negative mood is often expressed slowly, and the child may or may not be irregular in sleep, feeding, and bowel elimination. This is the child who typically stands at the edge of the group and clings quietly to her or his mother when taken to a store, a birthday party, or a child care program for the first time. If the child is pressured or pushed to join the group, the child's shyness immediately becomes worse. But if allowed to become accustomed to the new surroundings at her or his own pace, this child can gradually become an active happy member of the group.

Nine Temperament Traits (Stella Chess, 1990)

1. **Activity Level**: Amount of movement and bodily activity

High Activity:
The highly active child likes movement and to run around, they get upset if made to sit quietly for long periods of time. A highly active child needs lots of active play. If the group is engaged in some quiet activity, let this type of child move around from time to time.

Low Activity:
The lowly active child can sit quietly looking at books. They tend to move slowly. Because this child moves slowly, she or he is sometimes teased as a slowpoke. It is important to understand

that a child with this low activity level will need extra time to get things done, such as dressing or moving from one place to another.

2. **Biological Rhythms:** Regularity or irregularity of such functions as sleep/wake cycle, hunger, and bowel elimination.

Regularity:

The regular child has a consistent, regular schedule each day, such as sleeping through the night, naps, eating and bowel movements. There are no problems with eating or sleeping and is easily toilet trained.

Irregularity:

The irregular child is the opposite; sleep and feeding vary, they may wake up several times a night, they may not eat on a regular schedule, and bowel movements are unpredictable. Toilet training may be difficult as the child needs to learn to be consciously aware of the sensations of elimination.

3. **Approach/Withdrawal:** How the child responds to a new situation or other stimulus.

Approach:

The child who is able to approach can reach for new toys, smile at strangers and responds positively to new foods. This child presents few problems to the caregiver, except when combined with high activity, in which case they may act impulsively or explore dangerous objects.

Withdrawal:

The child who withdraws will be cautious when exploring new objects and may spit out new food. When taking this child to new places they may cry or strain to get away. To help the child overcome his reluctance, provide small and repeated exposures to the unfamiliar.

4. **Adaptability***:* How quickly or slowly the child adapts to a change in routine or overcomes an initial negative response.

High Adaptability:

The high adaptability child adjusts easily to new situations and schedules. Such a child does not usually present a problem to the caregiver.

Low Adaptability:

The low adaptability child takes a longer time to adjust to change or a new situation. They can be misjudged as stubborn or uncooperative. Pressuring the child to adapt quickly will only boomerang and have the opposite effect.**5**

5. **Quality of Mood**: The amount of pleasant, cheerful and openly friendly behavior (positive mood) as contrasted with fussing, crying, and openly showing unfriendliness (negative mood).

Positive Mood: The child whose mood is positive is open and easily pleased. They are usually laughing and smiling.

Negative Mood: The child whose mood is negative tends to fuss or complain a lot, even at trivial discomforts, and may cry before going to sleep. The child may show little or no open expression of pleasure. Ignoring the child's negative mood helps them to respond positively.

6. **Intensity of Reactions:** The energy level of mood expression, whether it is positive or negative.

Low Intensity:

The low-intensity child expresses in a low-key way both pleasure and discomfort. When happy the child may smile, if upset the child may fuss and whine, but not loudly.

High Intensity:

By contrast, the high-intensity child expresses her or his feelings with great intensity. When happy, this child bubbles and laughs; when upset, cries loudly and may even have a tantrum. The caregiver will need to evaluate whether the issue is trivial or important.

7. **Sensitivity Threshold**: How sensitive the child is to potentially irritating stimuli.

Low Threshold:

The child with a low threshold may be easily upset by bright lights, loud noises, change in temperature and a wet or soiled diaper. This child may not be able to tolerate rough texture or tight clothing. The caregiver needs to be aware of these issues and attend to those reactions, but not try to change them.

High Threshold:

The high threshold child does not feel irritated or uncomfortable, and it does not bother them to sit in a wet or soiled diaper. The caregiver needs to regularly check to see if the infant has a wet or soiled diaper to avoid diaper rash.

8. **Distractibility:** How easily the child can be distracted from an activity like feeding or playing by some unexpected stimulus, such as the ringing of a telephone or someone entering the room.

High Distractibility:

The highly distractible child is easily distracted by sounds or other objects. In older children, high distractibility may not be such a desirable trait.

Low Distractibility: The child who has a low distractibility can focus on an activity despite other noises and distractions. But low distractibility creates a problem if the child is intent on trying to reach a hot stove and is not easily diverted. In a case like this, the child may have to be removed from the situation.

9. **Persistence/Attention Span:** Two closely related traits, with persistence referring to how long a child will stay with a difficult activity without giving up, and attention span referring to how long the child will concentrate before her or his interest shifts.

High Persistence:

The highly persistent child can be absorbed in what she or he is doing for long periods of time.

The child may get upset if forced to quit their activity when in the middle of it. Warning a child in advance will help with the transition. The highly persistent child, even after a firm no, may continue to badger or plea for more time.

Low Persistence:

The child with low persistence and a short attention span will not stick with a task that is difficult or requires a long period of concentration. Later in childhood a short attention span and lack of persistence make learning at school and home difficult.

Goodness of Fit

Goodness of fit refers to how well the child's temperament matches with their environment. Some environments and temperaments fit together, while others do not. The teacher who understands the difference in temperament and *goodness of fit* is more apt to support the child's social and emotional development. Understanding the theory of *goodness of fit* can help a teacher decide if changes may be needed to better match the child and their environment. Selecting activities that "fit" the child can help them feel more successful, develop a trusting respectful relationship and raise the child's self-esteem. *Goodness of fit* provides the teacher with the ability to approach the situation with more empathy and help the child manage their reactions to the environment. Since children and adults have their own behavioral styles and temperaments, it is important to know and understand both the child's temperament and how they respond to situations and know your own temperament and how you respond to the child.

Temperament Theory in an Early Childhood Classroom

Understanding the three temperaments and the nine traits that influence the relationships between children and adults and how the different traits require different approaches is pivotal to developing healthy emotional growth in children.

Exercise:

1. How can you implement Jean Piaget's theory in the classroom?

2. How can you implement Lev Vygotsky's theory in the classroom?

3. How can you implement Erik Erikson's theory in the classroom?

4. How can you implement Abraham Maslow's theory in the classroom?

5. How can you implement Howard Gardner's theory in the classroom?

6. What are your thoughts on Sara Simlanskys Play theory?

7. Explain ways you create an attachment to an infant?

8. What are some ways to create "Goodness of Fit" with a child?

Ingredient # 3 Creating a Safe Environment

"People will forget what you said, people will forget what you did, but people will never forget how you made them feel."

Maya Angelou

Safe Environment

According to Abraham Maslow's theory, when physical security and safety, including sleep, are challenged, students will use most of their time, energy, and creativity simply trying to survive. This ongoing struggle interferes with learning. Just, as an adult will experience anxiety from a constant level of stress, so will a child. However, it is often not recognized in a young child. Children need structure and routine, both in the home and at school, and they need to know what is expected from them in order for them to feel safe and to manage their emotions during their time away from home.

It is the teacher's responsibility to create a safe environment by providing a structured predictable classroom where the children can take risks and not be ridiculed or teased. The unknown can be anxiety producing for anyone, but especially for a child. A predictable structured, routine removes the fear of the unknown and allows the child to feel safe. Creating a safe and structured environment provides the opportunity for children to develop confidence and manage their behaviors, especially at the times when unavoidable circumstances arise.

Structure allows the child to internalize constructive habits.

Infants tell us what they need, they let us know when they are hungry, need to be changed or when they want to be held and comforted. In a relatively short amount of time they adjust to a routine of their own, which doesn't always meet the adult's routine. Expecting an infant to adapt to an adult's schedule is not realistic and will only create confusion and a feeling of unsafety for the infant when their needs are not being met.

Routine

Without routine our days would be a humble jumble of chaos! No one would know when it is mealtime, sleep time, school, work, etc. There would be a mass state of confusion.

A routine eliminates power struggles between child and teacher and helps a child develop a sense of responsibility. The child comes to learn there are specific times of the day that certain activities are necessary, i.e. circle time, center time, outside time, brushing teeth and preparing for sleep, meal time, etc. Providing a visual daily schedule at the child's eye level will help the child feel safe and learn the structure of the routine.

There is less stress and anxiety with a visually consistent routine. Children are more likely to cooperate when they know what is expected and at what times, they will feel more in control of their activities, and will become more independent and less likely to be oppositional.

Choices

While providing a structured routine, it is also necessary to allow children to make choices throughout their day. Choices allow children to feel in control.

According to Erickson's theory, he believed that at the second level of psychosocial development, beginning soon after one year of age, young children must resolve the conflict between autonomy and shame and doubt. Children who do not develop autonomy are liable to remain dependent on adults or to be overly influenced by peers (Erikson, 1950). Learning to be autonomous and self-reliant takes time and practice. When we offer children choices, we are allowing them to practice the skills of independence and responsibility, while we guard their health and safety by controlling and monitoring the options (Maxim 1997).

A child's self-esteem grows when they are able to do things for themselves and when they feel they are taking part in decision making. Offering a child a choice helps them to feel empowered, it enhances their thinking ability, and aids in problem solving, thus, avoiding power struggles. The more a child is given the chance to participate in making a decision for themselves, the more they develop autonomy. Being autonomous and in control feels good, and that feeling helps the child to take the needs of others into consideration when making choices (Kamili, 1982). The more children are offered choices, the less conflict there is in the classroom. When an adult continually denies the child the chance to participate in decision making, the more likely it is that the child will not develop the natural feeling of independence and may become rebellious. This behavior may be seen as challenging, and the child will be viewed as having a behavior problem.

When allowing a child to make a choice, it needs to be meaningful to the child and acceptable to the adult. As an example, if two children are arguing over the same puzzle, the teacher might suggest sharing the puzzle together, or the teacher can offer to help one of the children find another puzzle to use. It is best not to offer too many choices which can overwhelm a child and limit their options. Making a choice is a skill for which the child needs time, support, and practice. Of course, there are times when there is no choice due to a safety issue or a regulation.

A teacher who practices the Peaceful Classroom Recipe understands that children make choices throughout the day. Even when their choice is to disobey, defy rules or ignore the teacher, it is still a choice on the part of the child. It is the responsibility of the teacher to help the child make appropriate decisions and to accept the choice they made. In so doing, we help to develop confident and independent children who feel in control of themselves.

Classroom Guidelines

There is a difference between rules and guidelines. Rules tend to be of a more demanding, negative nature, and start with the word "No," i.e. No hitting. No running. Guidelines, on the other hand, have a more positive tone and state the behavior you want the child to observe.

Examples:

- Inside voices

- Listening ears

- Eyes on teacher

- Friendly touches, hands on our own bodies

- Walking feet

- Kind words to our friends

- Words to solve problems

Children have more respect for rules when they are permitted to actively participate in creating them. They develop a more meaningful sense of community and cooperation. Young children who are not ready to take part in creating guidelines feel more connected when the guideline is discussed and explained to them in simple terms. Discussing why a guideline is important helps the child to understand the significance of a guideline and why they sometimes may not always remember to follow it, and what they can do when they forget and make a mistake (Gartell, 2003).

Teachers who commit time and effort to the process have found it benefits children's relationships and increases understanding of what it means to participate as a constructive member of a classroom community (Castle & Rogers, 1993).

Transitions

Transitions can be stressful on children when they are asked to shift from one activity to another in a relatively short amount of time. For many children, transiting times often create confusion and stress and out of control behavior. The teacher needs to incorporate transitions within the daily routine. Having planned active transitions prevents an out of control classroom and helps to eliminate possible behavior problems.

General Practices for Transitions

Provide children sufficient time to prepare for transitioning from one activity to another. Some children need time to mentally prepare for the changes and to feel more in control. Children who have a difficult time during transitions will need to be closely monitored. They may need simple directions with only one or two commands at a time.

Minimize the amount of time that children need to wait for the next activity. Waiting in line creates boredom, and boredom invites pushing, shoving and inappropriate behavior. To avoid the negative behavior, the teacher could make the transition fun by utilizing songs, finger plays, puppets and simple games. Transition time offers opportunities for learning, problem-solving, following directions and cooperation.

Some Ideas for Easy Transitions

- Songs
- Finger plays
- Have children move like a certain animal
- Clapping games
- Memory games
- Puppets to give directions
- Children wiggle different parts of their bodies
- Identify things in the classroom that start with certain letters
- Relaxation techniques- Pizza breathing
- BE CREATIVE- the more CREATIVE the better the cooperation from the children

Incorporating fun, interactive transitions into your routine will eliminate many behavior problems.

Exercise:

1. Are you incorporating transitions into your daily routine?

2. What do your transitions look like in your classroom?

3. Do you have a visual schedule hung up at child's eye level?

4. Observe your classroom wait time, are you noticing challenging behaviors at this time? If so what behaviors are you observing?

5. Have established classroom guidelines for classroom with the children?

6. Do you review your guidelines daily?

7. How do you feel about offering children choices?

8. How do you offer choices?

Ingredient #4: Communication Skills 101

"The biggest communication problem is we do not listen to understand, we listen to reply."
Steven Covey

Communication

Communication is between two or more people, one is the speaker and the other or others are the listener. The listener is as important as how well the speaker is able to communicate their thoughts. Communication goes beyond the use of words; it includes the tone of voice and body language. Teachers in particular need to be aware of their choice of words and how those words are being said. Often our own personal emotional state develops into a negative habit. Psychiatrist William Glasser (Glasser, 1998). coins the term the "Seven Deadly Habits." **These include:**

1. Criticizing
2. Blaming
3. Complaining
4. Nagging
5. Threatening
6. Punishing
7. Bribing, rewarding to control

By becoming aware of our speech, we can refrain from using negative habits to positive habits, known as Glasser's "Seven Caring Habits."

1. Encouraging
2. Listening
3. Supporting
4. Accepting
5. Trusting

6. Respecting
7. Negotiating differences

Communication Speaker/Listener

When speaking it is best to direct the statement as an "I-message or as an I-statement" which is an assertion of the speaker's feelings, such as "I feel…". In the "I-message or I-statement" the sentence begins with "I". Keeping the message in the "I" prevents the listener from becoming defensive. Everyone is entitled to their own feelings, which are neither right nor wrong, simply an individual's personal feeling. When communicating, it is not necessary to agree on every matter, but it is important to accept the other's point of view.

In contrast to the "I-message or I-statement" the "you-message or you-statement begins with "you". "You….."

Speaker "I-Message"

I feel…………………………… when you……………………………………..

Active Listening

Listening is the most fundamental component of interpersonal communication skills. Hearing is not the same as listening. To be an effective active listener, the listener needs to remain silent and focused on what is being said without interrupting, interjecting, looking away, or being distracted. Active listening requires patience to allow the speaker a moment to explore their thoughts and feelings. Hearing is different from listening. The same letters that are in *Listen* are in *Silent.*

Non-Verbal Active Listening

Individuals who are actively listening often display non-verbal signs. They look directly at the speaker and show a genuine sense of interest, they lean forward or tilt their head, or nod their head in affirmation to what is being said, or they mirror-reflect the speaker with facial expressions of sympathy, empathy, or with a smile.

Verbal Active Listening

There are several ways the listener can demonstrate that what the speaker said was heard and understood. Validation shows the point of view was understood; asking questions to clarify what was said; expressing an understanding ("I understand what you are feeling"); repeating or paraphrasing in order to show comprehension. All are powerful skills that can reinforce the message of the speaker.

Communication in the Classroom

Communication begins right from birth by speaking softly, and singing and humming lullabies. The few moments it takes to change a diaper provides the perfect opportunity to engage in happy talk and to bond. During the period language skills are developing is an opportune time to start modeling effective communication proficiency. Teachers can play an important role in developing the child's communication skills. Children learn by example. How an adult expresses themselves and how well they are listened to will help the child understand the importance of communication.

Children communicate by:
- Crying
- Smiling

- Cooing
- Babbling
- Gesturing
- Single words
- Sentences
- Drawing
- Writing

When a child comes to the teacher to talk or with a conflict, the first thing a teacher needs to do is role model active listening and resist the urge to jump in and solve the issue or disregard what they are saying.

1. **Actively listen to the child:** come to the child's eye level by either kneeling or sitting in order for them to make eye contact, demonstrate that you are listening by nodding your head or confirming you hear what they are saying, and allow the child to finish their thoughts. When they are finished, ask questions to further engage them in conversation.

2. **Confirm that the child is listening:** when speaking to the child, ask them to pay close attention to what is being said. It is important for the child to understand the significance of listening to others. When you are finished speaking, ask the child to repeat in their own words what was said. Praise them for good listening.

3. **Limit interruptions:** Children need to be taught to allow others to express themselves without interrupting. A positive way to curb impulsive interruptions is the use of a *"talking Stick."* A *"talking stick"* is a special stick that the children can help decorate. Whoever is holding the stick is the only one who may speak. This teaches self-control, respect and listening skills. The stick can be used during any exchange of communication, such as a conflict or circle time.

Simple activities like the teacher reading a story or playing a game of Simon Says can help children develop keen listening skills while enjoying a fun experience.

Tips for Communication in the Classroom

- Make requests and directives clear, firm and always friendly.
- Keep the request simple and short. When the child is following the request utilize specific feedback.
- Be aware of tone and body language, be respectful and non-judgmental.
- A simple rule to follow is: "Say what you mean, mean what you say, and don't say it mean."
- Dr. Julie Jochum implemented the concept of the "compliment sandwich", two positives per negative. The two slices of bread are the positive statements, and the filling of the sandwich is the correction. The compliment sandwich provides a focused way of giving encouragement. The technique is useful with children for preventing or resolving problems. It is important to positively connect with the child first before offering a correction. Example: "John you have put away all the blocks, now put the cars in the bin, and then you are all set."
- Communicate in a positive manner, not a negative one, i.e., no running, use walking feet.
- Use the "I-message or I-statement". "When you….I feel…"
- Allow for a response time.
- Before responding, check in that you are calm.
- Don't take what the child says personally.
- Keep direction short and to the point; multi-steps need to be broken down.
- Make use of the "talking stick" to limit interruptions.
- Sing to the children.
- Scaffold language by elaborating and extending what children say.
- Engage in one-on-one conversation.

- Talk to the children, not at them.

Effective communication skills are needed in every type of relationship with children, parents, co-workers, administration and strangers. Most conflicts arise because there was not clear communication. The speaker was not explicit, or the listener was not listening. Teachers need to develop their own communication skills first in order for them to adequately model for children. Effective communication can alter the climate of the classroom.

Exercise:

- Observe your communication skills over the week with both co-workers and children.

- Review the seven deadly habits. Do you identify with any of them?

- Replace the negatives with the seven caring habits.

- Practice the "I message" statements for a week.

- Practice the compliment sandwich for a week.

- Observe if you feel a shift in the classroom environment, when utilizing the compliment sandwich theory.

Ingredient # 5: Intentional Connection

"Connection is the energy that is created between people when they feel seen, heard, and valued."
Brene Brown

Connection

Connection begins with you and your own self-awareness. That will allow you to connect with children and promote their learning. You want to connect, not control. Children can read the meaning in the sound of your voice, your facial expressions and body language.

Relationships are the active ingredient for learning. Having relationships is the foundation for all growth. Strong connections are made through positive interactions. When an early childhood educator develops a strong connection, it allows the child to feel safe. Strong connections are made intentionally through descriptive encouragement, active listening, engaging in the moment, and asking open ended questions. Each time an early educator interacts with a child, it helps the child to learn and understand how they feel about themselves.

Children learn best when they experience positive relationships. When early educators are more responsive and engaged in the child's interest, the child's cognitive development is stimulated, which helps them to become more confident and excited to learn.

Teachers who intentionally plan interactions with children help them to develop a sense of safety and wellbeing. The sound of a teacher's voice, the words that are chosen, and a smiling face are some of the ways to help form connections with children. The teacher who takes the time and demonstrates an interest in the children helps to stimulate a child's imagination and develop a broader vocabulary.

A good way to connect is making use of Dr. Stanley Greenspan's Floor Time Theory. With infants, teachers can connect by getting down on the floor at their level and in their space. The teacher/caregiver can utilize every opportunity throughout the day to connect: diapering and feeding present the perfect time to connect. *Floor time* meets children where they are. It provides quality time for the teacher and child to interact with one another. As children get older and feel more connected, they are more apt to be inspired, curious, and creative which enhances them intellectually and emotionally.

Quality time means being present in the moment, quieting the mind, and consciously interacting with the child. Making time interacting with each child every day helps build a warm, safe relationship. Without quantity, there is no quality in a relationship.

Regardless of the child's age, the teacher can join in the child's world, can challenge and inspire them to be creative, and can widen the interaction to encompass their senses, motor skills and emotions.

Encouragement vs. Praise

There is a difference between encouragement and praise. Encouragement empowers the efforts of the child, while praise gives approval to the achievements (Hitz & Driscoll, 1988). When praise is strong, children become anxious about the possibility of not living up to the adults' expectations (Kohn, 1999). Encouragement offers hope and incentive.

Teachers who encourage children by commenting on how hard the child worked or how much they improved help to develop the child's self-esteem and inspire them to work. Descriptive encouragement builds confidence, there is no judgment involved, and it focuses on the child's effort, even if the child failed at the task. The child feels proud of their own accomplishment, not defeated by failure. Encourage the process not the end result.

Examples of a descriptive encouraging statement would be, "Look at all the yellow you used in your painting, how beautiful."; "I bet you are proud of the building you made with the blocks."; "You shared your doll, thank you."

Catch Them Being Good

As soon as the teacher witnesses a child making use of appropriate behavior, acknowledge the behavior with positive encouragement. Positive encouragement fosters more positive behavior. Teachers can easily become distracted with all the bustling and activity in the classroom, and not notice, or miss an opportunity to mention when witnessing a child using appropriate behavior. Teachers who offer more positive reinforcement rather than negative attention deepen the connection with the children and create a safe, loving environment.

Ask Open Ended Questions

There are two types of questions; the open ended and closed ended. The closed ended questions can be answered with a yes or a no. They often begin with Did you? Do you want to? Will you? Have you? The open-ended question cannot be answered in a one-word reply, such as yes or no. They usually begin with what, how, who and why. The open-ended question actively involves the child and fosters conversation, improves their vocabulary, and stimulates their imagination to answer in more descriptive details. The open-ended question allows the child to feel what they have to say is important, which builds the connection between child and teacher. When the child does not feel connected they may seek attention in a negative way, preferring negative interaction to no interaction. When a child is engaged in challenging behaviors, this child needs the most connection from you.

Take the time to catch them being good and give them immediate descriptive encouragement. This will help to build the relationship and encourage cooperation. Before the behavior can improve, there needs to be a connection, a sense of trust and a level of respect between the child and the teacher.

A teacher is on the go from the moment the children arrive to the moment they leave. Throughout the busyness of the day allow some time to slow down and enjoy the interactions with the children. Powerful interactions can make a difference throughout a child's life. Children flourish in environments where they are encouraged and supported.

Exercise:

- Do you really listen, if so how?

- Do you give a child time to share, if so how?

- Do you brush off what the child is saying in order to move on to your own agenda, is so how can you change that behavior?

- Do you come to work and count the hours until you can go home?

- Are you a curious, ongoing learner?

- Do you encourage children to problem solve, if so how?

- Do you genuinely recognize accomplishments and challenges, if so how?

- Do you often feel you're on automatic pilot?

- Do you pay close attention to what the children are doing or saying, or are you simply going through the motions?

- Are you always thinking about what's next instead of what is happening now?

Ingredient #6: Social Emotional Learning

"Treat others the way you want to be treated."

Golden Rule

Social Emotional Learning

Although we are born as social beings with the need to intermingle and be around others, social skills are also learned and need time to develop. Social skills begin with the bonding of parents, interaction with siblings, playing with other children and becoming a part of a larger community through school and other social gatherings. Social abilities change over the course of a lifetime. Each aspect of developmental growth (social, physical, emotional and language cognition) is connected and can affect one another. For example, a child's language skills increase so does their ability to verbalize their feelings.

The environment a child grows up in and their early emotional experiences set the foundation in developing social and emotional skills. Children who start school in an emotionally supportive environment will acquire the love of learning necessary for success in all areas of school. "As young children develop, their early emotional experiences literally become embedded in the architecture of their brains; therefore, great care should be given to children's emotional needs. All children benefit from social-emotional learning programming, but the benefits are even greater for children with delays in social-emotional skill development associated with early socioeconomic disadvantage." (Bierman, K.L., Morris, P.A., & Abenavoli, R.M, 2016).

Social Milestones Chart (retrieved from NACCRRA, 2008):

Infants 0-1	Toddlers 1-3	Preschoolers 3-4
Responds to touch and sound	Imitates adult behavior in their play	Starts being able to share toys
Turns head towards sound	Engages in simple pretend play, talking on telephone	Watches other children play, joins in the play
Establishes eye contact	Follows simple directions, waves bye - bye	Has friendships with other children
Smiles when spoken to	Displays assertiveness by saying "no"	Participates in associative play
Smiles at self in mirror	Displays aggressive feelings and behaviors	Is concerned about the feelings of others
Plays pee-a-boo and patty cake games	Watches other children in their play	Helpful cleaning up toys
Displays different emotions	Participates in small group activities, singing and dancing	Requests permission for activities and items

Social-emotional development is defined by three main areas of a child's social-emotional

learning regulation:

1. Acting
2. Feeling
3. Thinking
4.

Acting: Behaving in socially appropriate ways that enhance learning.

- Interacting with teachers and peers in positive ways by sharing and taking turns.

- Solving problems with increasing independence.
- Negotiating solutions to conflicts with peers.
- Inhibiting negative impulses (e.g., hitting, pushing, yelling).

Feeling: Understanding others emotions and regulation of own emotions.

- Accurately identifying emotions in their social-emotional learnings with others.
- Managing strong emotions such as excitement, anger, frustration and distress.
- Being empathetic and understanding others' perspectives.

Thinking: Regulating attention and thought.

- Focusing attention on a lesson or an activity.
- Screening distractions.
- Planning steps or strategies to complete a task or activity.

Helping Children Express Their Feelings

- Naming and identifying feelings: children need help identifying their feelings and putting a word to that feeling. Placing a name to a feeling helps the child develop an emotional vocabulary so they are able to verbalize feelings.

  Ask the children to talk about their feelings and what they think another child might be feeling.

- Talking about feelings: tell the children what makes you feel angry, sad, happy, or any other emotion, and how you express that feeling. Ask them what makes them feel angry, sad, etc., and how they let people know what they are feeling. Using picture books or an "emotion" poster or cards is an excellent way to illustrate emotions and get the children talking about their feelings and help them come up with solutions. Talk about feelings throughout the day, when playing games, or while in groups. The more a child has the chance to notice what they are feeling and to talk about the feeling, the quicker they will learn.

Role of the Teacher

The teacher can naturally promote social-emotional development and problem-solving skills throughout the course of the day by implementing social skills in their curriculum activities, and by engaging children to find a solution to a social conflict or a challenging situation. Teachers will want to focus on *the interpersonal skills,* such as getting along with others, making friends, sharing, cooperating, taking turns and controlling aggressive behavior. This includes emotion regulation such as identifying and managing emotions, and developing empathy, focusing attention, and flexible problem solving (Durlak, J.A., Weissberg, R.P., Dymnicki, A.B., Taylor, R.D., & Shellinger, K.B., 2011). Because most children spend an increasing amount of time in child care, teachers have the opportunity to contribute to children's social-emotional learning in a variety of ways.

Six Ways to Support Social–Emotional Learning

1. Provide detailed instructions: Hold up an emotional expression picture card or point to an expression on the emotional poster and ask the children what the emotion is you are pointing to. If they respond with happy, ask how "happy" makes them feel. Or select a few children to point to a facial expression and ask what they are feeling at that moment.

Keep it simple. Social-emotional learning skills can be implemented throughout the day, such as while reading a story and asking the children how they think the character in the story is feeling.

2. Provide scaffolding: Teachers can help children develop their social-emotional skills by building upon what the children already know, such as the name of a basic emotion like feeling sad. Ask the children if they notice that one of their classmates is feeling sad, and what solution they could offer to help the classmate. As an example, "Anna seems sad that she wasn't included in the game. I bet Anna would feel better if she was asked to join in."

3. Learning through reading books: While reading a book to the children, ask if they ever felt the way the main character feels in the book. Use a variety of books that touch on feelings (decision making, problem solving, coping skills, impulse control, etc.).

4. Model rules and expectations: Children learn by imitating others, especially their teachers and their parents. Teachers can promote social-emotional learning by purposely modeling ways in which emotions are expressed and how they are regulated in social situations. This can be accomplished by letting the children know how you feel and what you're going to do about your feelings.

5. Validate and encourage the expression of feelings: Teachers can validate a child's feelings by asking what is wrong rather than telling the child to stop crying or whatever emotion they are exhibiting. When the teacher understands why the child is upset, they can help the child understand the emotion they are feeling and help provide a solution.

Dismissing a child's feelings does not provide the chance for the child to learn how to cope and acknowledge those emotions.

6. Guide children toward reflection: It is important for children to understand their emotions, what causes them, and how to obtain relief. This is an important element for children to develop such traits as altruism and empathy later in life. You can let the child know that you witnessed him/her being kind to his/her classmate and by offering the classmate a hug. You can ask how it felt to be kind.

The environment in an early childhood classroom is one filled with busyness and activity and often emotionally-charged. Children are sponges, absorbing and noticing everything that goes on around them during the day. They are continually learning social and emotional skills in their daily interactions with teachers and other children, while in the classroom or on the playground and continuing at home with parents and siblings. The daily guidance and education from parents and teachers prepares children for kindergarten and beyond.

Exercise:

1. What social-emotional activities are you incorporating into your day and how? Explain in detail.

2. Explain why social-emotional learning is so important in the classroom for young children?

Dr. Tamara Pelosi

Ingredient #7: Conflict Resolution

"Problems cannot be solved with the same mindset that created them."

Albert Einstein

The definition of mediation or conflict resolution: the act of balancing power.

Children view a problem from their own perspective and in the immediate moment. It takes time, practice and experience for children to develop conflict resolution skills. Three of the most common sources of conflict are property, privilege and territory. The young child is more likely to react when they feel another child has taken something they feel is theirs (property), when another child is coming into what they view as "their" territory, or if they believe another child has privileges they don't have. Young children do not like to share (property/territory) or take turns (privilege).

Everyday incidents present opportunities for teachers to help children resolve conflicts and can be viewed as teachable moments. Explain to the children that you are going to start using problem solving in the classroom to help them to come up with solutions and solve their problems. You can designate a special puppet to introduce this new concept.

The use of the *calm down center* and the *talking stick* are excellent tools for helping even the youngest preschooler develop important lifelong skills. If your classroom does not allow you to have a calm down center, then designate a table that you can name as the "Peace Table," where the children can go to resolve a problem. With the guidance and support from teachers, children learn how to resolve a conflict in a positive way. As their communication and active listening skills develop, so does their self-confidence and their ability to problem solve.

Before a conflict can be resolved, everyone, including the teacher needs to be calm (Ingredient #2 Self-awareness/calm). Children can be taken to the calm-down center and can start off with utilizing the pizza breathing technique.

Calm Down Center

- Sometimes the only way that teachers can help a child to calm down is by separating them from the situation.

- This cooling time is different from time out.

- Children can go to the calm down center to gain control of their emotions.

- The calm down center is a safe place for the children to learn from their mistakes, rather than punishing them for their mistakes.

Pizza Breathing

Pizza Breath - hold your hands out flat in front of you and make your hands into a pizza shape.

- Take a deep breath in and smell the pizza.
- Count to three and hold in the breath.
- Blow out the breath. Blow on the pizza, it is hot! Do this 3-5 times.

Puppets

Puppets are another conflict tool. Designate a special puppet to be the decision-making puppet.

This puppet can be part of the class. The puppet should be introduced when there isn't a conflict.

Puppets have a magical way about them; they come 'alive' to the children. The decision-making puppet helps the children to communicate and understand in their own language how to make better decisions and resolve conflicts.

Steps in Resolving Conflicts

Children need calm consistency, support, and repeated practice to resolve conflicts. With the guidance of teachers, children can learn to solve problems through simple steps. Teachers need to continually role model to support the steps (Adopted from High Scope).

Calm down

- Communicate in a calm, non-threatening manner.
- Immediately stop any unsafe or harmful action.
- Stand between the children in conflict.
- Take the matter to the calm down center to be discussed, away from distractions and interruptions.
- Validate the children's feelings by naming the feeling: sad, hurt, and angry ("I see that you are sad….").
- Use "mirror-talk", and let the children know you hear what they are saying.
- Both children and teacher need to be calm; nothing can be resolved without being calm.

Define "What is the problem"

- Gather the necessary information in order to identify the problem.
- Actively listen to what the children are saying and help them to explain the problem and put their feelings into words.

Brainstorm Solutions

- Teachers can ask the children how to solve the problem and encourage them to come up with a solution on their own.
- Teachers can offer supportive ideas in a non-judgmental way.
- Demonstrate you are helping, not demanding.

Put the solution into effect

- Observe how the children are interacting.
- Provide descriptive encouragement to the children for resolving a conflict.
- If the solution not working, bring the children back to think of another solution.

With time and repeated practice, children can learn to use these steps to solve problems without the help of their teacher. Resolving conflicts helps children learn valuable communication skills and can encourage them to be more accepting of different points of view. Problem solving is a complex skill and needs constant practice before it can be a learned skill.

Exercise:

1. How do you feel about implementing conflict resolution in your classroom?

2. Can you designate an area for solving problems? Such as the Calm Down Center.

3. How will you introduce Conflict Resolution to the children?

4. Designate a classroom decision making puppet and talking stick.

Ingredient #8: Understanding Behaviors

"Kindness should become the natural way of life, not the exception."
Buddha

Understanding Challenging Behaviors

It is definitely a challenge for early educators to spend many hours of their day struggling with behavior problems in their classrooms. They quickly become overwhelmed and develop a sense of hopelessness, they feel they have tried everything, and they don't know what else to do or who to ask.

Challenging behaviors are a normal course of development. All children experience defiance, hitting, pushing, yelling, grabbing, shoving, kicking, pinching, scratching, teasing, biting, not wanting to share, tantrums, tattling, impulsive behaviors, attention difficulties, hyperactivity and difficulty with transitions. These are all normal. Physical aggression is common in the one-two-year old stage as a means of expressing their frustration, anger, fear and sadness. The two-three-year old is still in the egocentric stage, it is all about them and everything is "mine." Sharing of classroom toys does not come easy at this stage, neither does understanding. It is quite common that many of these behaviors will be exhibited in the classroom setting due to a child's lack of social and language skills, or inability to control emotions or understand verbal and non-verbal cues. Now take into consideration that these little ones are left every day without their main source of comfort – their parent.

A complete background is necessary to determine the many risk factors that can contribute to challenging behavior, starting with the birth of a child, or any illnesses or injuries during childhood, and including the environment the child grows up in.

Risk Factors Associated with Challenging Behaviors:

Biological Risk Factors
- Premature Birth
- Trauma at Birth
- Fetal Alcohol Syndrome
- High Risk Pregnancy
- Drug use during pregnancy
- Speech/Language Delays
- Developmental Delays
- Auditory Processing
- Sensory processing
- ADHD/Neurobiological condition

Physical Risk Factors
- Lack of proper nutrition
- Dehydration
- Illness
- Lack of medical care
- Allergies
- Accidents/injury
- Pain (chronic or acute)

Record any behavior observed to determine if any of the physical risk factors come into play.

Emotional Risk Factors

Temperament:

- Easy/Flexible Child

- Difficult/Feisty Child (Teachers may have a difficult time with this temperament)
- Slow-to-Warm-Up/Fearful Child
- Anger: Help the child to release their anger appropriately.
- Anxiety: A child needs to feel safe in their environment; establish clear boundaries, structure and predictability.
- Over-stimulation: Children cannot process what is going on around them when they are over-stimulated.
- Need for attention: A child will look for attention in any way they can; negative attention is better than no attention.
- Need for control: To help a child feel in control, offer appropriate choices.
- Frustration: Provide coping skills when the child begins to feel frustrated.
- Jealousy
- Defiance
- Low Self-Esteem

Family Environment Risk Factors

- Move to new location
- Serious illness or death of parent or guardian
- Parents/guardians with demanding work schedules
- Inconsistent/inadequate parenting
- Substance abuse
- Divorce
- Domestic violence
- Poverty/poor housing/unsafe living conditions

- Overly controlling/overly disciplined
- Abuse/neglect

There is not much a teacher can do to change a child's family environment risk factors, unless there is abuse (then it would get reported) but understanding those risk factors will help in being compassionate and non-judgmental.

Classroom Environment Risk Factor

- Unsafe environment, both physically and emotionally
- Excessive noise and stimulation
- Unrealistic expectations
- Inconsistency in daily schedules
- Unclear guidelines
- Unplanned/unexpected transitions
- Excessive use of the word "no"
- Imbalance of directions to children
- Insufficient duplicate toys

Four concepts that contribute to challenging behavior:

1. Challenging behavior is a symptom of an underlying cause
2. Behavior is communication
3. Behavior has a goal
4. Behavior occurs in patterns

Behavior is a symptom of underlying cause:

A child's exhibiting of a challenging or maladaptive behavior is a symptom of an underdeveloped skill, which is often a lack in coping strategies or the inability to communicate their feelings of anger, frustration or anxiety. These children act out in inappropriate, disruptive or aggressive behaviors. It is difficult for a teacher to be empathetic to these children, often viewing the child's behavior as purposeful, rather than understanding the child's needs. Some children are sensitive to a stressful environment and overreact with a fight or flight response. There can be overreaction to small setbacks or changes. These children are lacking the social skills needed to respond appropriately (Minahan & Rappaport, 2016).

Behavior is means of communication:

All challenging behavior is a means of communication and is the result of a child not having the skills to handle a specific situation or expectation. However, as their brain evolves and their language and attention span increases, they are more able to control their emotions, and begin to learn how to express their feelings and needs.

Just because a child can start to communicate doesn't mean they have the skills to show how they feel. When a child becomes agitated and irrational and does not have the skills to express their feelings appropriately, they are more likely to kick, push, scream, growl, bite, or do whatever it takes to get someone to listen.

Each behavior tells us something; it has a purpose, it is goal directed, and it attempts to meet the child's needs. Identifying the goal of the behavior by understanding the purpose reduces the possible misinterpretation of the behavior and gives a chance to teach alternative behaviors.

Behavior has a goal:

- **Attention seeking:** Feeling disconnected. The child will do whatever they can, either negative or positive, to gain the recognition they feel they deserve.

- **Avoidance:** Feeling frustrated. Because of an inadequate skill, as Dr. Ross Greene states, "behaviors come from a lagging skill or an unsolved problem."

- **Power/control:** Feeling powerless. The child may not follow directions and be argumentative.

- **Revenge:** Feeling hurt. The child may treat others cruelly or bully them.

- **Sensory Input:** Some children with sensory difficulties who have trouble with the sensory input from the environment can become overwhelmed. They try to mask the uncomfortable input through different, more pleasing sensory-seeking behaviors (Minahan & Rappaport, 2016).

Challenging behaviors occur when the demands or expectations exceed a child's capacity to respond adaptively or appropriately at that time. When children are getting their message across in an inappropriate manner is not the time for the teacher to be judgmental and punish, but rather to be curious and discover the pattern and the underlying function of the behavior. Look beyond the challenging behavior and ask yourself, "What is the child trying to say? And what does the child really need?"

Behaviors happen in patterns:

It is often perplexing for a teacher to understand where a behavior is coming from or what triggered a particular behavior. Every behavior has a starting point. Infants cry and fuss to get their message across, but older children, although able to speak, still resort to behavior to express themselves. The teacher needs to do a little detective work to discover the reason for the behavior. Is the child looking for attention? Trying to avoid a situation? Seeking sensory, or are they overstimulated? There is a reason and explanation for all behavior. A child quickly learns that a tantrum or any negative behavior easily gets them what they want. A child who behaves in a way that elicits negative responses usually does so because negative attention is more efficient, faster and easier to obtain. The behavior is intense, dramatic, and can verify the child's existing poor self-image. The negative attention only reinforces their low self-esteem, which results in the self-fulfilling prophecy, and creates a vicious cycle.

Once the teacher understands the reasons for the challenging behavior, and what triggers the behavior, they are more readily equipped to intervene without reinforcing the negative behavior, by responding differently and helping the child shift the negative learned behavior with a proactive approach.

Exercise:

1. Make a commitment to yourself to view challenging behaviors through the lens of: there is no such thing as a "bad" child, just a child who needs help in resolving their challenges.

Ingredient # 9- Problem Solving Challenging Behaviors

"A child whose behavior pushes you away is a child who needs connection before anything else."
Kelly Bartlett

Challenging Behaviors

Challenging behaviors are indicative of a child with a problem and, all too often, they are labeled as a difficult child. A favorite quote by Dan Gartell is, "There is no such thing as a bad kid, only kids with bad problems that need help in resolving them." It takes investigating to learn why the child is behaving inappropriately. When the behavior is understood, it can be stopped and prevented by teaching the child the necessary skill.

The only behavior a teacher can control is their own. I have discovered the most important way to help teachers feel empowered is to help them be more self-aware and reflective of their thoughts and attitudes, and how their behavior can improve the child's behavior. As teachers become more aware of their own reactions or responses and reflect on what is going on in the classroom environment, they may also discover some of the contributing factors in problem behavior.

Some questions for teachers to consider:

- Are the popular centers too small or not equipped to accommodate enough children?
- Is the room physically and psychologically safe?
- Are there too many teacher-directed activities?

- Is there enough variety of engaging materials?
- Is the classroom overstimulating?
- Is the routine not clear and consistent?
- Do the children need to wait too long?
- Are the children given choices?
- Is there sufficient time in their day for ample movement?
- Are any of the teaching practices contributing to the behaviors?
- Is more attention given to a child when they act negative?
- Are expectations too high?
- Are you letting yourself be drawn into a power struggle?

Anyone of these can contribute to challenging behaviors.

Up until this point of the book I have focused on the proactive ingredients, such as knowledge in brain development, child development, self-awareness, providing guide lines that contribute to a safe and consistent routine, communication skills, descriptive encouragement, choices, conflict resolution skills, and gaining the understanding that behaviors are a form of communication that need to be discovered. It is not about controlling behavior; it is about gaining a relationship and making a connection. It is about becoming an investigator and figuring out why the behavior is happening, and how you as the teacher can model and teach new skills.

The good news is that challenging behavior can be changed. Trying to manage the negative behavior will not teach the skills needed to create a change. Remember, changing behaviors takes dedication, time, patience, and consistency. The longer the child has been displaying the problem behavior, the longer it may take to change it. Each new skill needs to be modeled, encouraged, praised, and practiced with lots of repetition in order to make the new skill permanent.

Intervention Strategies for Challenging Behaviors

During my research I discovered the many challenging behaviors that teachers experienced, such as tantrums/meltdowns, anger/aggression, defiance and impulsive acts. This chapter will explore each of the challenging behaviors and offer a strategy for that behavior.

As discussed in prior chapters, challenging behaviors are a normal course of development and a result of the child not having the skills to handle a specific situation or expectation. It's normal for young children, especially those in the one-two year stage, to be defiant and aggressive towards others when they are upset and trying to reach a goal. Since they are physically expressive and lack adequate receptive language skills, have difficulty verbalizing frustration, fear, and sadness, are not able to control their emotions or understand verbal and non-verbal cues, challenging behaviors are, therefore, observed at some time in a classroom. Physical aggression will continue until the child's brain develops and they gain the ability to control their emotions and learn to communicate. A challenging behavior is not to be seen as bad, but as a sign that the child is experiencing an emotional, social or physical predicament that is overwhelming. Without adult intervention these actions can develop into negative behavior patterns (maladaptive behaviors) and get caught in the negative loop.

Temper Tantrums

Although temper tantrums are normal for young children at the one-year to four-year old stage, they can be challenging to deal with, and frustrating for both teacher and parent. To understand a temper tantrum, we need to look at the human brain. The brain is divided into two sides; the right side of the brain governs feelings, symbols and images, while the left side of the brain governs logic, reasoning, order and language. Because the right side of the brain is more developed at this age level, children are more emotional and not able to reason or verbalize what they are feeling. Temper tantrums are often a result of feeling frustrated when the child is trying to do something beyond their capabilities, or as a means to obtain attention. Remember, negative attention is better than no attention. It is more likely for a child to have a temper tantrum when they are tired, over-stimulated or hungry.

Temper tantrums tend to subside as the child matures and develops language skills. However, even with the ability to communicate their feelings, they may still resort to a tantrum because they have learned that a tantrum quickly gets them what they want. Emotional outbursts may continue even without the child's desired result, as negative habits form to the dismay of both parent and teacher.

How to Respond to Temper Tantrums

There are three steps in handling tantrums:

1. Listen attentively to what the child is trying to express, and observe their facial expressions, their body language and their words.
2. Repeat back three or four times what the child said, mirroring the same words and feelings, letting them know their feelings are recognized. "I see you are so mad you cannot have that toy."

3. Once the toddler is calm, the teacher needs to help the child resolve the problem and give a big hug.

What Not to Do

1. Do not try to use reason with a toddler, or point out the child's error, as their brain is not mature enough for reasoning. Use the above steps to calm the child and resolve the problem.
2. Do not give in to the child and let them have the toy that they were not permitted to have or avoid the expected chore (putting away their toys). Giving in only reinforces the emotional outburst, gets the desired effect, and results in the child developing long term maladaptive behaviors.

Temper tantrums in children three and older stem from one or more of four situations:

1. When the child is told "no." Children do not like when they are told they cannot have something or are not able to do something. Instead of using negative commands, such as don't, stop, and not now, rephrase it with a positive word and an explanation.
2. Children become upset when they have to stop playing or participating in a fun activity. They need to know beforehand that there is a time limit, and that the teacher will let them know an activity will end in 15 minutes, 10 minutes, 5 minutes.
3. Offer a choice to a child when asked to do something they don't want to do.
4. Children resort to tantrums to get attention. Ignore the behavior unless the child is endangering himself or others.

Utilizing these steps of what to do and what not to do will not only help decrease the toddler's tantrums, but also teach the skills necessary for appropriate behavior.

Anger/Aggression

When children feel anxious, frustrated or angry, they resort to hitting, kicking, spitting, biting or any other aggressive behavior. They don't have the skills to solve their problem, cope with stress or express their feelings. Teachers need to remain calm, discover the reason for the behavior, and help the child with a resolution.

Common Reasons Why Children Get Angry and How to Respond

Retrieved from "Top 10 Reasons Why Kids Get Angry" (Lively, 2017)

Become aware of what was going on in and around the child prior to their outburst.

1. The child is tired, hungry or over-stimulated. Were they showing signs of fatigue? Were they agitated and irritable? Had they had their snack/lunch? Had their room or activity been too loud with too much stimulation? Even if environments don't bother you, they may temporarily overload the child's system.

   - How to respond: Provide a quiet rest time for the child who is tired. A child who is sensitive to low blood sugar may get very grumpy when they are hungry. Give them a quick snack to take the edge off to help diffuse the effect of over stimulation. Offer a quiet space for activities such as playdough, drawing, coloring, soft music or a story to calm down the overloaded system.

2. The child feels disconnected: Before the child got angry were they overly clingy, or nagging? Were you annoyed by their behavior?

   - How to respond: Empathize with how they are feeling and spend more quality time connecting with the child.

3. The child feels powerless: A sign of powerlessness is anger; you will hear "No", "I don't want that", or you see refusal to cooperate and power struggles.

   - How to respond: Give ample choices and responsibilities to help them feel more independent. Refuse to engage in the power struggle. Allow the child to participate in decision-making.

4. The child feels hurt: Young children are not capable of expressing their feelings and want to hurt back, become aggressive or say hurtful words to whomever they are angry at.

   - How to respond: Empathize with the source of their anger. "You look really angry. Are your feelings hurt? Did someone say something to hurt your feelings? That can make you feel very angry." When the child has calmed down, let them know it's okay to feel angry, but not okay to name-call or hit to show it. Teach the "I-statement" to express how they are feeling.

5. The child's boundaries have been invaded: Children, like adults, have their own set of boundaries. Either their physical space has been invaded, or their personal space. Not every child wants to be hugged or kissed and may respond angrily.

   - How to respond: Teach the child to state their boundaries clearly by using the "I-statement."

6. The child feels anxious: Children often react with anger when feeling anxious or fearful. The child does not want to appear frightened; anger/aggression gives the child a feeling of being in control.

   - How to respond: After the outburst is over, talk to them about how they were feeling before they got angry.

7. The child is frustrated by not getting what they want: The usual reaction when a child is disappointed in not getting what they want is to have a temper tantrum. If the temper tantrum works, the child will continue to have them and get the results they desire.

   - How to respond: Do not give in to the tantrum, acknowledge the child's feelings, provide a choice and a coping skill. Through this the child will learn that tantrums do not give the desired result.

8. The child feels frustrated because they are not able to communicate what they want or what they need. Do you give the child sufficient time to tell you what they want? Often a child becomes so excited to talk about something they stutter and stumble over their words. A very young child or a child with verbal delays may lash out when not able to get their message across.

- How to respond: Acknowledge the child's feelings, and if you can, teach sign language. It helps with children who cannot verbally communicate.

9. The child is displacing their anger: Outbursts may seem sudden and unexpected, but had been building up throughout the day, perhaps due to a situation with a friend or family member that happened earlier. Suppressed emotions accumulate until the child is over-tired and overstressed before the outburst occurs.

    - How to respond: Know it is not your fault, they are tired from the long day. Help them label the anger, empathize, listen, and help them find a healthy outlet for the tension.

10. The child feels unheard or misunderstood. When a child is trying to tell you something, and they feel you aren't understanding or listening to what they are saying.

    - How to respond: Use the communication skills you have learned and acknowledge what they are saying by mirroring back what they say.

Diffusing Tactics for Challenging Behavior (Prysor-Jones, 2017)

Teachers need to practice how to respond to situations and not react to them. De-escalation techniques and remaining calm are not an overnight process. They are skills that require patience and practice. Reasoning with an angry child does not work. The goal is to reduce the level of agitation in order for problem solving to take place. Teachers who know and understand the children in their classroom, especially the child with behavior challenges, will be more successful in de-escalating the situation before it becomes out of control. One of the most important tools for a teacher is learning to recognize the signs, i.e., how a child "tells," by certain behaviors that precede the meltdown.

Early signs that should not be ignored:

- Refusing to speak or a steady repeating of "no"
- Speaking rapidly and loudly
- Clenching their jaw/tensing their body/head thrust forward
- Shaking/trembling/fidgeting
- Avoiding eye contact
- Grunting/grumbling/mumbling
- Hiding
- Looking menacingly at another child

Non-verbal strategies:

- Relaxed body language: shoulders/jaw relaxed. Calm can be just as contagious as fear. Approximately 55% of what we communicate is through physiology, 38% is through the tone of our voice and just 7% is through the words that we use (Prysor-Jones).
- Get down to the child's height by sitting or kneeling so as not to intimidate the child.
- Find a safe quiet place away from staring eyes.
- Model a calm manner for the child to copy.

Verbal strategies:

- Divert the child's attention away from the cause of contention.
- Keep your voice calm and low.
- Use positive words in your request, "If you join us in line, I will help you put your boots on."
- Help the child to express what they are feeling. If child won't talk, use a visual picture to encourage communication.
- Keep your statements simple with few words.

Ask the child, "Are you ready to listen?" Questions should not be asked if a child is hurting himself or anyone else, or if the child is being destructive. But they can be asked when the child is yelling, stamping their feet, or refusing to look at you. Wait for the child's answer. If the child replies with a "no", tell the child when they are ready to listen they can sit down alongside you. When they answer "yes", thank the child for listening and calmly redirect them to the matter, "It's time to line up", or It's time to put toys away."

- Stick to your initial concern, and do **not** shift your focus to secondary behaviors unless they are dangerous or cause a problem. Once the initial concern is resolved, if the secondary behavior is still continuing, ask yourself the following questions:

  - Is it dangerous?
  - Is it creating a problem for the other children?
  - Is it creating a problem for me?
  - If the answer to the questions above is no, the secondary behavior can be addressed another time when the child has not escalated.
  - If the answer is yes, address the secondary behavior.

Stop dangerous or hurting behaviors every time as soon as you see them. When the child is calm, give them a simple direction to get them back on task behavior. This may lead to an escalation in the moment, but the benefit is it teaches the children in the class they are safe with you and that you will help them when they feel out of control. When the child is successfully on task again, let the child know you will check in with them in a few minutes to see that they are still using on task behaviors.

Defiance

It is extremely frustrating when a child willfully refuses to do what is asked and answers even the gentlest request with a flat out "no"! There is something about a child looking you straight in the eye and saying, "No, I won't do that," "I hate you," or "You can't make me," that can challenge one to the core. Children are defiant when they feel disconnected and lack control. Often defiance results in the child receiving the attention they crave, even when that attention is negative. Teachers need to be on guard not to become enmeshed in a power struggle in an attempt to gain control over the situation and prove that you're the boss. Unfortunately, it is the teacher who will lose. The teacher needs to remain in control, rather than to control. The goal is not to control the child, but to teach the child self-control. As soon as you observe the signs of possible defiance, you will need to redirect the child with gentle reminders before the situation escalates and you lose control.

Ways to deal with defiance

It is important to build a positive connection, especially for children who act defiantly. The more the child pushes you away, the more that child needs your connection. Build the relationship. Reinforce their progress and effort with specific encouragement. Whenever possible make a point of noticing the child's successes, big and small, in following directions, transitioning smoothly, or doing anything that ordinarily might invite resistance. When you know a child is resistant, be proactive and offer choices. Providing opportunities for the child to make their own choices allows them to exercise their newfound autonomy.

Once you have given the appropriate reminders or redirection, physically step back to give the child more space - literally and emotionally. Most children need a few minutes to decide what to do; allow them the time to do this. Expecting a child to immediately comply will only lead to more resistance. Children know how to push our buttons. Teachers need to keep their emotions in control and not take the behavior personally. When you understand that the child's behavior is about their feeling a lack of connection, you are more apt to direct the child away from defiance.

Impulse/Self-control

Trust is a necessary component for self-control. Teachers who portray a caring, kind demeanor and acknowledge the child's needs, gain the trust of the child. A teacher who is able to control their own emotions and reactions is an excellent role model for helping children learn how to regulate their emotions.

Self-control is learning to control the mind, which needs to be developed in children. Children who have not yet mastered this quality may exhibit the following:

- Difficulty waiting their turn
- Is aggressive toward other children – pushing, hitting, kicking
- Difficulty in following rules
- Easily becomes frustrated and angry
- Grabs toys and games away from other children
- Behaves inappropriately to get attention
- Does not comprehend the consequences of their actions

Skills needed for developing self-control and impulse control:

- Social skills
- Attention and memory skills
- Awareness of feelings
- Problem-solving skills
- Verbal language skills

As children develop and are more involved with other children by playing games and sharing toys, they ultimately learn how to control their emotions and impulses.

Strategies that can help children learn how to control impulsive behaviors:

- **Exercise:** Both physical exercise that raises the cardiovascular and mindful exercise such as yoga are the best ways to reduce stress for everyone, especially children. Exercise helps to change the function and structure of the pre-frontal cortex of the brain.

- **Identifying and communicating feelings:** Ask what the child is feeling and suggest words to help them verbalize that feeling, i.e., Are you mad? Scared? Angry? Ask where they feel it in their body, i.e., In the head? Belly? Heart feels like it is beating fast? Try to help the child identify what caused the feeling, i.e., another child took the toy? The child was pushed? Assisting the child to understand the cause of the feeling will help them be more capable of self-control.

- **Playing games:**

  "Freeze game:" A fun way for children to release energy. Children dance when the music plays and freeze when it stops. Dance quickly for fast-tempo songs, slowly for slow-tempo songs.

  Follow the musician: Children play musical instruments whenever the teacher waves her hands, increasing and decreasing the tempo, and the children either slow down or speed up.

  Clapping hands: The teacher claps hands with a certain tempo and the children imitate the tempo.

Strategies for Emotional Regulation:

- **Counting to Ten:** The teacher faces the class with her arms raised high above her head and her fingers wide open, and slowly counts from one to ten. As she is counting she lowers her arms down alongside her body. The children imitate the teacher's actions and count along with her.

- **Pizza Breath:** Ask the children to hold their hands out flat in front of them as if they had a pizza on their hands. Ask them to take a deep breath in and smell the pizza. Count to three, hold in the breath, then blow out the breath. Tell the children the pizza is hot so they have to repeat this a few times.

- **Calming Imagery:** Ask the children to lie down on the floor on their backs with their arms alongside their body, their legs stretched out and their eyes closed. Quietly ask them to imagine that their body is feeling very, very heavy, that their toes feel heavy, their feet feel heavy, slowly moving up the body, mentioning belly, back, arms, etc. Then ask them to imagine they are laying on the beach on a warm sunny day, imagining a soft breeze and all the sounds around them, the waves washing up and back, the seagulls squawking in the distance. Once you notice that the children are feeling calm ask them to quietly sit up and open their eyes. This calming exercise will help them be more centered and focused.

ABC Log:

The A-B-C Log is an assessment tool used to look at a child's environment in order to determine what is the underlying cause of a particular behavior, and what the appropriate behavior goals and patterns will be implemented for that behavior. The teacher uses the assessment log to record the *antecedents, behaviors and consequences* for a week or two, approximately 15- 20 incidents. Collecting this vital data will assist in developing an individual plan by incorporating preventive practices and provide the proper intervention strategies required for the child's behavior.

- **Antecedents**
- **Behavior**
- **Consequence**

A. **Antecedents** are the conditions or triggers that immediately precede the occurrence of the child's behavior, including the time of day, settings, transitions, structure, needing attention, or any activity that either occurs or is present before the child exhibits challenging behavior.

B. **Behavior** refers to the child's challenging behavior. Log all behaviors noting what the child is doing, what does the child look like, how often does the behavior occur, how long does the behavior last, and what is the intensity of the behavior. When making your list, describe the who, what, when and where. Be detailed and specific.

C. **Consequence** refers to the events that immediately follow the occurrence of the child's challenging behavior. How was the adult responding to the child's behavior and what was the result of the behavior?

Children struggle to communicate their emotions. The action of a behavior is either to gain something or get away from doing something. It is the teacher's responsibility to interpret and interrupt the negative patterns, not simply by stopping the pattern, but by modeling, teaching, guiding, and helping the child develop the appropriate skills that will negate the negative behavior. Recall when a child is trying to get his/her message across is not the time to punish, rather it is the moment to discover the underlying cause in order to determine the reason for the behavior.

The Behavior Log is an excellent tool in detecting the triggers that cause the challenging behaviors. It helps the teacher focus more on **why** the child acted a certain way, rather than **what** the child did and what can be done about it. Be persistent in keeping detailed records. Be objective and only record what you see; do not add in assumptions or opinions. After several weeks of observing and recording behaviors you will be able to identify the triggers and recognize the patterns. This information will guide you to create strategies, and the appropriate interventions to prevent future behaviors. When creating intervention strategies, the goal is to teach and model the child for the appropriate way for him to get his needs met. You want to replace the negative behavior with the appropriate positive behavior. Sometimes, when implementing new intervention strategies, the behavior may worsen before it improves. Stay calm, confident, and stick with it. It will be worth it.

Individual Plan

After ABC's are compiled and the triggers have determined the underlying function of the behavior, develop support strategies for preventing future challenging behaviors. Design an individual plan for each behavior and how you will intervene in the behavior. Once this is completed and a plan has been decided, meet with the parents and let them know the intervention strategies you are implementing. You will need to remain professional, reporting only the facts. Do not express your personal opinion and remain non-judgmental and empathetic. Ask the parents if the behavior happens at home. It is important to build a relationship with all the parents, but especially the parents of children with challenging behaviors. If after a few months your intervention strategies are not working, you can have a second meeting with the parents. This is a very **delicate** topic. It is the not the role of the teacher to diagnose or voice your opinion. It is the time to review the strategies you have implemented and explain the reasons they are not working, such as the child may need additional support. You can inform the parents about Early Intervention or Preschool Evaluation process. You may need to meet with the parents several times until the parent is able to fully comprehend the severity of the situation. A referral for an assessment by special education may be part of the individual plan.

When teachers and parents collaborate and work together as a team, the groundwork is set for an effective problem-solving strategy to improve the wellbeing of a child who is having difficulties. This is an investment in the child's future.

The wise chef understands the relation of spices and how each spice enhances the flavor of the other. If even one is omitted, there is a lack to the taste buds. This book uses the same approach. Each of the positive, enriching ingredients need to be a part of the recipe in order to create a peaceful classroom.

When a child is displaying a challenging behavior in your classroom, take out your recipe and identify what ingredient is lacking. Think of challenging behaviors as opportunities to teach a child a new skill. Handling challenging behaviors gets easier and more productive when you take on a matter-of-fact mind-set and don't take the child's challenging behavior personally.

The Recipe to Create a Peaceful Classroom was designed to teach you how to be the *chef* of a Peaceful Classroom.

It has been my passion to guide early educators based on my own experiences and the knowledge I have gained along the way. You can turn your classroom's challenging behaviors into a Peaceful Classroom.

Recipe for Creating a Peaceful Classroom

Ingredients

1. Power/Self-Awareness/Calm
2. Richly Rooted in Knowledge
3. Creating a Safe Environment
4. Communication Skills 101
5. Intentional Connection
6. Social & Emotional Learning
7. Conflict Resolution
8. Understanding Challenging Behaviors
9. Problem Solving Challenging Behaviors

Exercise:

1. Keep your recipe handy and continue to check in on your ingredients.

2. For two weeks complete an ABC Behavior Log on a child who is displaying challenging behaviors in the classroom to identify the pattern and the underlying function. Once that is determined, create an individual plan with your administrator and the family.

ABC Behavior Log

Name _____ Class _____

Teacher_____

Description of Behavior

_____
_____
_____
_____
_____
_____
_____

Date	Time	Antecedents	Behavior	Consequence	Comments

Dr. Tamara Pelosi has twenty-five years of experience working with populations ages three to eighteen, along with their families. Within the twenty-five years of her career she earned her Doctorate of Education in Youth and Family Studies with a concentration in Special Education.

In 1992 she co-founded "Sunshine Prevention Center," a youth and family center which is located in Port Jefferson Station, New York. Dr. Pelosi was responsible for creating and teaching programs that were based on the community's needs.

Her doctoral dissertation was titled "*Increasing Social-Emotional Skills in Aggressive Preschoolers by Training Preschool Teachers in an Improved Teaching Methodology.*" For over a year she was dedicated to the study of why children had challenging behaviors and what were the functions of those behaviors. This research helped her to create intervention strategies and prevention techniques for a comprehensive teacher training program titled "Peaceful Classroom." Dr. Pelosi also founded Polaris Coaching and Consultant Services which offers a variety of coaching assistance, including Education and Guidance for Early Childhood Educators who are confronted with challenging behaviors in the classroom, ADHD Parent Coaching, and Woman's Empowerment seminars and workshops.

Dr. Pelosi has been the recipient of numerous awards attesting to her charitable character and her dedication to children and their families.

References

Bierman, K.L., Morris, P.A., Abenavoli, R.M. (2017). *Parent engagement practices improve outcomes for preschool children.* Edna Bennett Pierce Prevention Research Center, Pennsylvania State University.

Bowlby J (1988). *A Secure Base: Parent-Child Attachment and Healthy Human Development. Tavistock professional book.* London: Routledge.

Ainsworth, M. and Bowlby, J. (1965). *Child Care and the Growth of Love.* London: Penguin Books.

Bryant, D., Vizzard, L.H. , Willoughby, M., & Kupersmidt, J. (2000). A review of interventions for preschoolers with aggressive and disruptive behaviors. *Early Education and Development, 10,* 46-68.

California Department of Education and WestEd Center for Child and Family Studies. (2011). *California Infant/Toddler Learning and Development Foundations.* Sacramento: California Department of Education.

Castle, K., & Roger, K. (1993). Rule-creating in a constructivist classroom community. *Childhood Education, 70(2),* 74-80.

Center for Early Education and Development 2001: https://developingchild.harvard.edu/resources/three-core-concepts. Harvard, University.

Cheney, D., & Barringer, C. (1995). Teacher competence, student diversity, and staff training for the inclusion of middle schools students with emotional and behavioral disorders. *Journal of Emotional and Behavioral Disorders, 3,* 174-182.

Chess. S. (1990) Retrieved from: *Temperaments of infants and toddlers: A guide to social-emotional development.* California Department of Education.

Chess, S., & Thomas, A., (1996). *Temperament theory and practice:* New York, New York: Brunner/Mazel.

Diamond, M, & Hopson, J., (1998). *Enrichment Key to children's intelligence and creativity:* New York, New York: Plum/Penguin.

Durlak, J.A., Weissberg, R.P., Dymnicki, A.B., Taylor, R.D., & Shellinger, K.B. (2011.) The impact of enhancing students' social and emotional learning: A meta-analysis of school-based universal interventions. *Child Development, 82,* 405-432.

Erikson, E. (1950). *Childhood and society.* New York: W.W. Norton.

Gardner, H. (1999). *Intelligence reframed: Multiple intelligences for the 21st century.* New York: Basic Books.

Gartrell, D. J. (2004). *A guidance approach for the encouraging classroom (3rd ed.).* Clifton Park, New York: Delmar Learning.

Glasser, W. (1999). *Choice theory: A new psychology of personal freedom.* New York: Harper Collins.

Green, R. (2014). *The explosive child: A new approach for understanding and parenting easily frustrated, chronically inflexible children.* New York: Harper Collins.

Greenspan, S. (1985). *First feelings: Milestones in emotional development of your baby and child.* New York: Penquin.

Goldman, D. (1995). *Emotional intelligence.* New York: Random House.

High Scope (2017). Retrieved from: https://highscope.org/curriculum/preschool/details

Hitz, R., & Driscoll, A. (1988). Praise or encouragement? New insights into praise: Implications for early childhood teachers. *Young Children, 43(4),* 6-13.

Hung, D. & Nichani, M. (2002). https://schoolworkhelper.net/important-early-childhood-educators-jean-piaget-lev-vygotsky/

Jochum, J. (1991). Responding to writing and to the writer. *Intervention, 26(3),* 152-157.

Kamii, C. (1982). *Number in preschool and kindergarten.* Washington, DC: NAEYC.

Kohn, A. (1999). *How children fail.* New York: Pitman.

Ledoux, J. (1996). *The emotional brain, fear, and amygdala.* New York: Simon & Schuster.

Lively, S. (2017). Top 10 reasons why kids get angry. *One Time Through.* Web 2 May.

Maxim, G.W. (1997). *The very young: Developmental education for the early years,* 5th Ed. Upper Saddle River, NJ: Merrill/Prentice Hall.

Maslow, A. (2017) Retrieved from: https://en.wikipedia.org/wiki/Abraham_Maslow

Minahan, J. & Rappaport, N. (2016). *The behavior code: A practical guide to understanding and teaching the most challenging students.* Massachusetts. Harvard Education Press.
Piaget, J. (1960). *The moral judgment of the child.* Glencoe, IL: Free Press.

Prysor-Jones, E.(2017) Using de-escalation techniques effectively. Web 8 March.

National Association of Child Care Resource & referral Agencies, NACCRRA. (2008) Daily Parent New York, New York.

Ruiz, D.(1997). *The four agreements: A practical guide to personal freedom.* California, Amber-Allen Publishing.

Shore, R. (1997). What we have learned in rethinking the brain. New York: *Families & Work Institute.*

Siegel, D. & Bryson, T. (2012). *The whole brain child: 12 revolutionary strategies to nurture your child's developing mind.* New York: Batman Books.

Slavin, R.E. (2005). *Educational psychology: theory and practice.* Needham Heights, MA: Allyn and Bacon.

Smilansky, Sara; Shefatya, Leah (1990). Facilitating Play. Gaithersburg, MD: Psychosocial & Educational Publications.

Vygotsky, L. (1987). *Thinking and speech: The collected works of Vygotsky.* New York: Plenum.

Wood, K.C. (2008). Piaget's Stages. Retrieved April 25, 2009, from Department of Educational Psychology and Instructional Technology, University of Georgia Web site: http://projects.coe.uga.edu/eplt .

Zero to Three (2004) Infant & Early Childhood Development Fact Sheet. https://www.zerotothree.org.

Command, -Demand = connet, reduuet

how r u feeling? @ circle time
uy book + picts
Sign languge feeling

Dr. Tamara Pelosi

Made in the USA
Middletown, DE
13 June 2019